Summer Smart
Between Grades 4 & 5

This book belongs to

_____

Published in the United States by Random House, Inc., New York, and in Canada by Random House of Canada Limited, Toronto.

A Penguin Random House Company.

The material in this workbook was previously published in _4th Grade Reading Comprehension Success_ and _4th Grade Math Games & Puzzles_ as trade paperbacks in 2009 and 2010, and as _4th Grade Vocabulary Flashcards_ and _4th Grade Math Flashcards_ in 2011 and 2013 by Sylvan Learning, Inc., an imprint of Penguin Random House, LLC.

www.sylvanlearning.com

Cover Design: Suzanne Lee
Summer Smart Interior Production: Big Yellow Taxi, Inc.

Original Workbook Credits:
Producer & Editorial Direction: The Linguistic Edge
Producer: TJ Trochlil McGreevy
Writer: Amy Kraft
Cover and Interior Illustrations: Shawn Finley and Duendes del Sur
Interior Photos: Jonathan Pozniak
Layout and Art Direction: SunDried Penguin

First Edition

ISBN: 978-0-525-56921-3
ISSN: 2639-9598

This book is available at special discounts for bulk purchases for sales promotions or premiums.
For more information, write to Special Markets/Premium Sales, 1745 Broadway, MD 6-2,
New York, New York 10019 or e-mail specialmarkets@randomhouse.com.

PRINTED IN THE UNITED STATES OF AMERICA

10 9 8 7 6 5 4 3 2

Say NO to Summer Slide and YES to Summer Smart!

Parents, you know that for kids, summer always seems to fly by without a care in the world (and hey—they deserve the break!). But research shows that if kids stop learning entirely over summer vacation, they can lose up to 2½ months' worth of knowledge from the previous grade through "summer learning loss." That's why we at Sylvan created the **Summer Smart Workbook** series!

By adding just a few pages per day into kids' summer routines, you can help your child keep their skills fresh and set them up for 5th grade academic success in the fall. Our **Summer Smart** workbooks bring you:

- Over 100 colorful pages of **fun, teacher-created learning exercises** that reinforce reading and math skills

- **Recommended summer book lists** (for both reading *and* math topics—yes, there are fun math books out there!), plus discussion questions to spark comprehension

- A **Vacation Challenge section full of bonus games and activities** that take learning off the page and into the real world

- Bonus **cut-out flashcards** to use for learning on the go

- A **"Summer Smart!" Achievement Certificate** you can display once your child has completed the workbook

Your child will love the great mix of activities, stories, and games in these pages. *You'll* love seeing their improved confidence and newfound love of learning. With **Sylvan Summer Smart**, you don't have to compromise between entertainment and education—instead, you can get a jump-start on making school a positive experience in the fall!

Thanks for choosing us to help foster the development of confident, well-prepared, independent learners!

The Sylvan Team

Here's what some families have shared about Sylvan workbooks:

"Using Sylvan workbooks helps my child keep an interest in school subjects while not in school. It helps keep his focus on the importance of learning even when outside his school environment. And it also helps me during those interminable 'I'm bored' days!" – *B.B. Lawson*

"My daughter has improved her academic skills and confidence while completing Sylvan workbooks. She also was excited to complete the Sylvan workbook pages, because they are engaging but challenging at the same time. She is looking forward to completing more pages throughout the summer to keep her skills up. Thank you, Sylvan, for this!" – *K. Haynes*

"[They] often include games and puzzles that are creative and educational, which helped my son, who doesn't like to study, brush up on skills, and even learn past his grade level! Sylvan is now part of my son's daily routine and eases up pressure and dependence on parents too." – *F. Mohamed*

Connect with your local Sylvan Learning Center and make an even bigger impact this summer!

Every child has the ability to learn, but sometimes children need help making it happen. Sylvan Learning uses a proven, personalized approach to building and mastering the learning skills needed to unlock your child's potential. Our in-center programs deliver unparalleled results that other supplemental education services simply can't match.

To learn more about Sylvan and our innovative in-center programs, call 1-800-EDUCATE or visit www.SylvanLearning.com. *With over 750 locations in North America, there's a Sylvan Learning Center near you!*

Contents

Contents

Section 1:
Summer Smart Reading

When you're getting ready to read, you should think ahead. Ask yourself what you think you'll find out. Then, when you're done reading, look and see if what you read had all the answers to your questions.

Say you're going to read this article: "200 Years of Bicycles."
Before you read, CHECK the box of each question you think this article will answer. (Don't try to answer the questions yet.) CROSS OUT the questions you don't think will be answered.

☐ 1. When were bicycles invented? _____

☐ 2. Who invented the wheel? _____

☐ 3. What was missing from the first bicycles?

_____

☐ 4. When was Susan B. Anthony born? _____

☐ 5. Why might bicycles replace cars? _____

_____

Now, READ the article.

200 Years of Bicycles

Bikes have come a long way since they were invented around 1818 in France. The first bicycles didn't even have pedals, you just pushed them along the ground with your feet! Now, almost 200 years later, we've got special bikes for roads, trails, and racing. Since bikes don't burn fuel or pollute the air, they may start to replace cars. Already, bicycles make up 40 percent of all traffic in the European city of Amsterdam. Even some American cities, like Portland, Oregon, are making cars give way to bikes on their streets. So start pedaling!

Go back and FILL IN the blanks in the questions you checked. Do you have all the answers? What about the questions you crossed out? Were you right?

✓ Check It!

Page 1

1. Around 1818.
2. X
3. Pedals.
4. X
5. They don't use fuel or cause pollution.

Page 2

Ask Questions!

1. 1895
2. X
3. 43
4. Asheville, North Carolina
5. X
6. Biltmore
7. 8000 acres
8. X
9. George Vanderbilt
10. X

Page 3

Ask Questions!

Suggestions:
-How long did it take to build?
-How much did it cost?
-What can you do for fun at Biltmore?
-What did Biltmore have that other homes of the time didn't have?

Page 4

Ask Questions!

1. Rocky Mountains
2. X
3. No
4. 150
5. X
6. 7–17
7. $3000 per session
8. X
9. Yes
10. Every night, weather permitting

1

Ask Questions!

Say you're going to read this article: "The Biggest Home in America."

Before you read, CHECK the box of each question you think this article will answer. CROSS OUT the questions you don't think will be answered.

☐ 1. When was the biggest home built?

_____

☐ 2. What is the capital of Kentucky?

_____

☐ 3. How many bathrooms does the biggest home have?

_____

☐ 4. Where is the biggest home in America?

_____

☐ 5. Did Ben Franklin really discover electricity?

_____

☐ 6. What is the biggest home called?

_____

☐ 7. How big is the backyard of the biggest home?

_____

☐ 8. Why can't penguins fly?

_____

☐ 9. Who built the biggest home?

_____

☐ 10. Is there a law that says kids can't stay up all night?

_____

Now, READ the article.

The Biggest Home in America

Would you like to live in the biggest home in America? Then head down to Asheville, North Carolina. That's where you'll find Biltmore—a palace built by millionaire George Vanderbilt in 1895. Don't forget to pack your swing set—Biltmore's backyard covers 8000 acres! And you'll need lots of toilet paper for the 43 bathrooms. There's also an indoor pool and bowling alley, just in case you get bored. The house took more than six years to build. No-one's sure how much it cost, but consider this: it had electric lights, indoor bathrooms, central heating, and an elevator during a time when most people were still using outhouses and oil lamps!

Go back and FILL IN the blanks in the questions you checked. Do you have all the answers?

WRITE down three more questions that this article answers.

_____

_____

_____

_____

_____

1

Ask Questions!

Are you looking for a sleep-away camp? Read this brochure: "Be a Butterfly!"

Before you read, CHECK the box of each question you think this brochure will answer. CROSS OUT the questions you don't think will be answered.

☐ 1. Where is Camp Kimimela? _____

☐ 2. Are other camps better than Camp Kimimela? _____

☐ 3. Can I bring a cell phone to Camp Kimimela? _____

☐ 4. How many acres does Camp Kimimela cover? _____

☐ 5. Do lots of campers get homesick and leave Camp Kimimela? _____

☐ 6. How old are the campers? _____

☐ 7. How much does going to the camp cost? _____

☐ 8. How many kids have been injured at Camp Kimimela? _____

☐ 9. Can I play tennis and volleyball at Camp Kimimela? _____

☐ 10. When do they have campfires at Camp Kimimela? _____

Another question to ask yourself before reading is "What do I already know?" Then, when you're done reading, you can ask: "What did I learn?" Try it out!

First, READ the topic. Then FILL IN the What Do I Already Know? column. After that, you'll be ready to read!

Topic: Tomatoes

What Do I Already Know?

_____

_____

_____

_____

_____

_____

What Did I Learn?

_____

_____

_____

_____

_____

_____

There's Nothing Rotten about Tomatoes!

We all know that tomatoes are good for us. But did you know that tomatoes are actually fruit? That's right! Tomatoes contain seeds and grow from a flowering plant—just like a strawberry. But since the tomato isn't sweet, it's generally considered a vegetable. Here's another fact about tomatoes: Every August, a town in Spain hosts *La Tomatina*, a massive food fight using tons of rotten tomatoes. Sounds like fun—as long as you don't have to clean up afterward!

Time to GO BACK and FILL IN the What Did I Learn? column. CROSS OUT any facts in the first column you got wrong. See how this works?

2

Before & After Questions

FILL IN the What Do I Already Know? column.

Topic: The Solar System

What Do I Already Know?

_____

_____

_____

_____

_____

_____

_____

_____

_____

_____

_____

_____

_____

_____

_____

_____

_____

_____

What Did I Learn?

_____

_____

_____

_____

_____

_____

_____

_____

_____

_____

_____

_____

_____

_____

_____

_____

_____

_____

Now, READ the article.

Our Corner of the Universe

The solar system is nine planets and the sun, right? WRONG. There's a lot more going on in our little corner of the universe than you think.

First of all, there are only eight planets. Sorry, Pluto, but experts have decided that you're not really a planet. (That's okay, Earth still loves you!)

So the planets of the solar system are: Mercury (closest to the sun), then Venus, Earth, Mars, Jupiter, Saturn, and Neptune.

Pluto used to come last in the lineup. But now it's considered a *dwarf planet*, which means that it's not really big enough to count as a planet. Other dwarf planets are Ceres and Eris.

There's more to the solar system than just the planets. The sun, of course, is the largest object in the solar system. But the system also includes moons, comets, and asteroids.

Scientists have learned a lot about the biggest asteroids. There are three that have orbits close to Earth: Atens, Apollos, and Amors. There's also a huge *asteroid belt* between Mars and Jupiter. This "belt" is like a highway for lots of asteroids.

It may sound like the solar system is a crowded place. Not! There are millions (sometimes billions) of miles between the planets and asteroids. They don't call it "space" for nothing!

Did you learn anything? GO BACK and FILL IN the What Did I Learn? column.

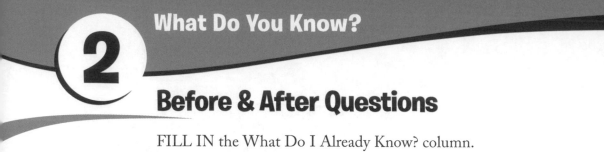

2

Before & After Questions

FILL IN the What Do I Already Know? column.

Topic: Fairies

What Do I Already Know?	What Did I Learn?
_____	_____

Now, READ the article.

Fairies: Fact & Fiction

There are lots of famous fairies in fiction. Where would Cinderella be without her fairy godmother? Or Peter Pan without Tinkerbell? Narnia is filled with fairies! Even more recent books, like *Artemis Fowl* and the *Spiderwick Chronicles*, are about people who try to learn all the secrets of the fairy world.

For hundreds of years, many people really believed in fairies. They blamed fairies for strange weather, natural wonders, or sudden illness. They thought naughty fairies like *brownies* and *pookahs* would steal objects or damage crops. Some thought bad fairies would take human babies and replace them with fairy babies (called *changelings*). They even blamed fairies when they got lost in the woods!

To get rid of fairies, people used iron, four-leaf clovers, or even bread. But not everybody disliked fairies. People who wanted to attract fairies built little houses for them to live in!

TURN the page to keep reading!

The most famous fairy story is, of course, about the tooth fairy. In the old days, some people believed that baby teeth were really powerful. They thought if a mean fairy took the teeth, she could work evil magic on the children. So, parents would bury their kids' teeth to keep them safe. Later, this practice changed to "burying" the tooth under a pillow or in a glass of water by the bed. Then, people thought the tooth fairy (a good fairy) would come and replace the tooth with money or a gift. This is a much nicer legend!

In 1917, two young girls took photographs of fairies flying around their backyard in Cottingley, England. The photos looked so real that people believed they were proof that fairies existed. Even the author of the *Sherlock Holmes* books, Sir Arthur Conan Doyle, was a believer! Years later, one of the girls confessed that all the pictures were fakes. The "fairies" were really cut out of paper. But in 2001, their photos sold for over $12,000!

There will always be people who want to believe in fairies. How about you?

Did you learn anything? GO BACK and FILL IN the What Did I Learn? column.

Get Ready to Read

PICK a new nonfiction book or article to read today. Before you start reading, FILL OUT this worksheet.

The title is _____

The topic is _____

_____

I think it will answer these questions _____

_____

_____

_____

_____

_____

_____

When you're done reading, CHECK all the questions that were answered. CROSS OUT the questions that weren't answered.

What other questions did it answer? _____

_____

_____

_____

_____

What Do You Know? What Did I Learn?

PICK a new nonfiction book or article to read today. Before you start, FILL OUT this worksheet.

The title is _____

Before you begin to read:

1. LOOK at the book cover or front page of the article.

2. SKIM through the story.

3. ASK yourself what you know about the subject.

What do I know?

1. _____

2. _____

3. _____

4. _____

5. _____

What did I learn?

1. _____

2. _____

3. _____

4. _____

5. _____

Sometimes authors are tricky. They like to write about things without actually telling you what those things are. Why? Because it makes you curious. It makes you read between the lines!

READ this story.

Timmy and the Truck

Timmy had lived at 328 Hampton Drive ever since he was little. It was an exciting place! Every now and then, a loud bell would ring, and all the men would drop what they were doing, slide down a pole, and jump on a big red truck. Then the truck would race out of the garage, lights blazing and siren screaming. Timmy wished he could ride the truck too. But he was always there when the truck came back, wagging his tail and barking "Hello!"

Now, CHECK the right answers, and FILL IN the blanks.

1. What's at 328 Hampton Drive?

☐ a. A dance club

☐ b. A Chinese restaurant

☐ c. A firehouse

How do you know?

_____

2. Who is Timmy?

☐ a. A fireman

☐ b. A little boy

☐ c. A fire dog

How do you know?

_____

See? You're too smart to let an author trick you. Let's do some more!

Check It!

Page 13

1. c: fire bell, fire pole, big red truck
2. c: wags tail and barks

Page 14

Check, Please!

1. c: same mom, Ophelia is two minutes older
2. a: front seat, pedaling, "backseat biker"

Page 15

Check, Please!

1. a: kids are dancing, yummy food
2. c: Zella is Red Riding Hood, Evan's a clown, Tory's a vampire
3. b: people moo at Amit and ask him for milk

Page 16

Author! Author!

Ask a friend to read your stories to try to read between the lines!

3

Check, Please!

READ this story.

> **On the Go**
>
> "I want to ride in front!" yelled Ophelia.
> "Too bad," said Felix. "I got on first."
> "But I'm the oldest."
> "Only by, like, two minutes. Get over it and start pedaling!"
> "Where are we going?" asked Ophelia.
> "To see Mom at her office," said Felix.
> "That's like three miles! We'll never make it!"
> "You're out of shape."
> "Watch out! You almost hit that cat."
> "Stop being a backseat biker!"

Now, CHECK the right answers, and FILL IN the blanks.

1. Who are Ophelia and Felix?

☐ a.   Best friends

☐ b.   Worst enemies

☐ c.   Twins

How do you know?

_____

2. What are they doing?

☐ a.   Riding a bicycle built for two

☐ b.   Driving a car

☐ c.   Riding their bikes

How do you know?

_____

Check, Please!

READ this story.

Moo!

Everyone was having a great time, except for Amit. Sure, there was yummy food, and some kids were dancing, but Amit was mad. His friend Zella looked great in her red riding hood, and Evan made a funny-looking clown. This only made Amit madder.

"What's wrong, Amit?" asked Tory, who was a vampire. "Aren't you having fun?"

"If one more person moos at me, or asks if I 'got milk,' I'm leaving!"

Tory laughed. "Poor Amit! Maybe you should have worn something else."

Now, CHECK the right answers, and FILL IN the blanks.

1. **Where is Amit?**

☐ a. At a party   ☐ b. In school   ☐ c. Selling candy door-to-door

How do you know?

_____

2. **What kind of party is it?**

☐ a. A birthday party   ☐ b. A slumber party   ☐ c. A costume party

How do you know?

_____

3. **What is Amit wearing?**

☐ a. A space suit   ☐ b. A cow costume   ☐ c. A wizard's hat

How do you know?

_____

3

Author! Author!

Now it's YOUR turn!

WRITE a conversation between a cat, a mouse, and a duck
without ever using the words *cat*, *mouse*, or *duck*. Make sure your reader knows who's who!

HINT: How would a cat talk to a mouse? Would a duck have a funny voice? What would their names
be? What do they look like?

_____

_____

_____

_____

_____

_____

_____

_____

_____

_____

_____

_____

_____

_____

_____

_____

You know the difference between a fact and an opinion, right? Did you know that they work together? Yep! If you've got an opinion, you should back it up with some facts. Check it out:

Question: Should kids have cell phones?

FILL IN some more facts to support each opinion.

OPINION	FACTS
YES	Kids can call parents in an emergency.
YES	Home phone lines aren't tied up.
YES	Kids can be more independent.
YES	_____
YES	_____
YES	_____
NO	Kids will use the phone too much.
NO	Phones and minutes are expensive.
NO	Kids could lose the phone or have it stolen.
NO	_____
NO	_____
NO	_____

Any time a news story or nonfiction article states an opinion, you should always look for the facts. Then you can make up your OWN mind!

✓ Check It!

Page 17

Suggestions:
YES:
1. Phones are cool.
2. Kids need to learn to use this essential gadget.
3. Kids can learn about managing money from the monthly bill.

NO:
1. Phones keep kids from socializing in person.
2. Phones keep kids from playing outside or exercising.
3. Phones in school or at the dinner table are bad manners.

Page 19

Suggestions:
YES:
1. Skaters can teach each other tricks.
2. Skaters could have a tournament.
3. Pietown could become famous for skateboarding.

NO:
1. It's not safe for kids who don't skate well.
2. Skater kids may misbehave.
3. It'll cost $5 to get in.

Page 22

Fact & Opinion

Suggestions:
YES:
1. Zoos have been around since 1793.
2. Animals are cared for in zoos: fed, safe, and healthy.
3. Scientists and the public learn a lot from animals in zoos.
4. Families can't see many animals in the wild.
5. Zoos breed endangered animals.

NO:
1. Animals aren't comfortable: there's no space.
2. Animals aren't behaving naturally in zoos.
3. Animals develop strange behaviors in zoos.
4. It's better to save the natural habitats of wild animals, because that helps the planet.
5. Only a few species have survived being born in captivity.

Q: Should Pieville open a skate park?

First, READ the news story.

New Skate Park on Mozzarella Street

Pietown is buzzing about Mayor Bixby Stiggle's plan to build a skate park next to the library.

"Pietown supports young athletes," said the mayor. "We provide basketball courts and baseball diamonds. A skate park is a logical next step."

"Why should those skater kids get a park? This town needs a good playground for toddlers first!" said Eva T. Finkle, who lives near the library.

Donald Sabin is pleased about the plan, but worried: "If it keeps skaters out of the empty pools in town, that's great. But is it safe for kids who don't skate well? And some of those skater kids are bad news. Will there be a grownup making sure everyone behaves?"

But his son DJ can't wait to try it out: "It'll be great to have a place just for skaters. It's a chance for us to get together and teach each other tricks. Maybe we can even have a tournament. Pietown could be famous for skateboarding!"

There is one thing that DJ doesn't like, though: The town will probably charge skaters $5 to enter the park.

Now, FILL IN the facts.

OPINION	FACTS
YES	The town builds other sports areas for kids, like baseball diamonds.
YES	It'll keep skaters out of the empty pools in town.
YES	_____
YES	_____
YES	_____
NO	Pietown needs a toddler playground first.
NO	It might not be safe for new skaters.
NO	_____
NO	_____
NO	_____

So? What do YOU think?

Should Pietown open a skatepark?

Circle one: YES   NO

Q: Should animals be kept in zoos?

First, READ the news story.

Concrete Jungle

People have been arguing about zoos ever since the first zoo opened to the public in 1793. It's a real knock-down, drag-out fight!

"Zoos are not comfortable for animals. In a zoo, birds have their wings clipped so they can't fly," says animal rights activist Mr. Leon Fribble. "And elephants, that often walk 20 to 30 miles a day, only have a little bit of space to move around."

Zookeepers don't agree. "Animals in zoos are fed every day, and they're safe from attack," says Mr. Hyram Higgins of the Pietown Zoo. "We even have doctors to take care of them when they're sick."

Plus, Higgins adds, "Not only do scientists learn a lot from animals in zoos, but ordinary people come every day to watch animals they would never normally see. It's a great lesson!"

But Fribble and other activists don't think that the chance for learning is worth keeping animals captive. "What are we learning?" Fribble asks. "These animals aren't living naturally. In the wild, their behavior is all about finding food. In zoos, they don't need to hunt, they don't need to make their own homes. They're not doing anything! Except maybe going a little crazy."

Fribble points out that animals living in small spaces, with humans constantly staring at them, can develop strange behaviors. For instance, animals might walk in the same circle all day long, or try to hurt themselves.

"Animals don't act like that in the wild. The only way you can learn about them is by watching them in their natural habitats," says Fribble.

But how many families can visit Africa to see a lion in the wild?

"We no longer live with many wild animals, like in the old days," says Higgins. "We've killed off most of the wolves and the bears and the buffalo. Zoos are our only chance to be near them."

The greatest benefit that zoos can give to animals is species preservation. Since the 1970s, zoos have worked hard to breed animals that are endangered. But their success has been limited. Only a few wild animals can survive being born and raised in captivity.

Some people think it would be better to preserve the animals' natural habitats.

"After all," says environmentalist Ms. Sindy Hoo. "If we save a jungle or a swamp, it's not just good for the animals that live there. It's good for the whole planet!"

Now, turn the page to FILL IN the facts.

Now, FILL IN the facts.

OPINION	FACTS
YES	_____
YES	_____
YES	_____
YES	_____
YES	_____
NO	_____
NO	_____
NO	_____
NO	_____
NO	_____

So? What do YOU think?

Should animals be kept in zoos?

Circle one: YES   NO

Read Between the Lines

CHOOSE a story to read, and try to catch when the author is being tricky— telling you stuff without saying it straight out. WRITE DOWN the clues.

Title of story _____

What is the author talking about? _____

_____

_____

_____

_____

What words does the author NOT use? _____

_____

_____

_____

So how did you figure it out? _____

_____

_____

_____

Fact & Opinion

PICK a new nonfiction story or book to read today. As you read, FILL OUT this worksheet.

Topic:_____

OPINIONS	FACTS
_____	_____
_____	_____
_____	_____
_____	_____
_____	_____
_____	_____
_____	_____
_____	_____
_____	_____
_____	_____
_____	_____
_____	_____
_____	_____
_____	_____
_____	_____
_____	_____
_____	_____

Skimming

They say a picture's worth a thousand words. Especially if it's a graph, a chart, or a map. When you're skimming an article, don't forget to slap your eyes on the pictures. SKIM this article.

HINT: Notice anything funny about this page? We've already blurred the words you can skip.

Pizza Time in Pietown

Pizza's Popular Seven Days a Week

Riusting ero euis auguer sed min laorger cilit, consequ ancorum e dio consectem doloreet num deli te digna feum ex eu faccum in et Riusting ero euis auguer sed min laorger cilit, consequ ancorum e dio consectem doloreet num deli te digna feum ex eu faccum in et

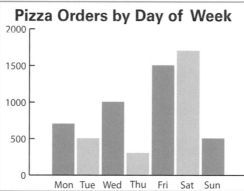

Friday and Saturday Rush!

Riusting ero euis auguer sed min ullao sacte velusting ero euis auguer sed mi laorger cilit, consequ ancorum ex auguer illarorger cilit, consequ ancorum dio consectem doloreet num deliquat aut lummdio consectem doloreet num de te digna feum ex eu faccum in et augiam.

Thursday Is NOT Pizza Night

Riusting ero euis auguer sed min ullao sacte velusting ero euis auguer sed mi laorger cilit, consequ ancorum ex auguer illarorger cilit, consequ ancorum dio consectem doloreet num deliquat aut lummdio consectem doloreet num del te digna feum ex eu faccum in et augiam.

Now, CIRCLE the right answers to these questions.

1. Which is the most popular night for pizza in Pietown?
   a. Monday   b. Saturday   c. Friday

2. Which two days had the same number of pizza deliveries?
   a. Friday and Saturday   b. Monday and Thursday
   c. Tuesday and Sunday

3. Which day has the least number of pizza deliveries?
   a. Thursday   b. Sunday   c. Friday

You can learn a lot from a graph like this. Let's try some more!

5

Skimming

SKIM this article.

Welcome to Pietown!

In Pietown, Pizza Rules

Riusting ero euis auguer sed min ullaor sacte wellusting ero euis auguer sed min ullaor laorger cllit, corsegu ancorum ex euguerc illaraorger cllit, corsegu ancorum ex eu dio corsectem doloreet num deliquat aut lummdo consectem doloreet num deliquat te digna feum ex eu facum in et augiam.

Pietown High: The Oldest Building in the State

Riusting ero euis auguer sed min ullaor sacte wellusting ero euis auguer sed min ullaor laorger cllit, corsegu ancorum ex euguerc illaraorger cllit, corsegu ancorum ex eu dio consectem doloreet num deliquat aut lummdo consectem doloreet num deliquat te digna feum ex eu facum in et augiam.

Pietown's Famous Purple Houses

Riusting ero euis auguer sed min iusting ero euis auguer sed min ullaor sacte vent laorger cllit, corsegu ancorum eaorger cllit, corsegu ancorum ex euguerc illanet dio consectem doloreet num deliqo consectem doloreet num deliquat aut lummodl ing ero euis auguer sed min ul er cllit, corsegu ancorum ex orsectem doloreet num deliqu ero euis auguer sed min ullao cllit, corsegu ancorum ex eu ectem doloreet num deliquat a feum ex eu facum in et augia auguer sed min ullaor sacte w egu ancorum ex euguerc illan loreet num deliquat aut lumm eu facum in et augiam.

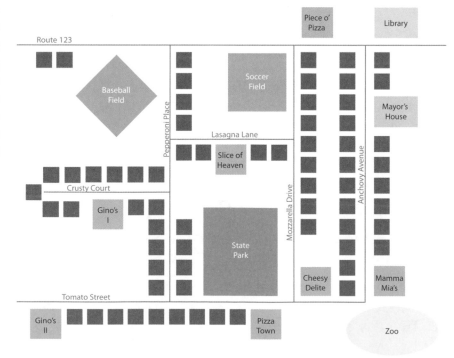

1. Which street do you take to get from Gino's II to Pizzatown?

   a. Tomato Street

   b. Route 123

   c. Anchovy Avenue

2. Which street is the longest?

   a. Route 123

   b. Pepperoni Place

   c. Lasagna Lane

3. What makes Pietown's houses so famous?

   a. They're really big.

   b. They're shaped like pizzas.

   c. They're purple.

4. What street should you live on if you don't want to be near any sports?

   a. Anchovy Avenue

   b. Crusty Court

   c. Mozarella Drive

5. What's the closest pizza place to the Pietown High?

   a. Pizza Town

   b. Gino's I

   c. Slice of Heaven

READ each question, and CHECK the right answer.

6. Which street does not have a pizza place?

   a. Route 123

   b. Lasagna Lane

   c. Pepperoni Place

7. How many pizza places do you pass when you go from the library to the high school?

   a. One

   B. Two

   c. Four

8. Which is the oldest building in the state?

   a. The Mayor's House

   b. Pietown High

   c. Mama Mia Pizzeria

9. To which pizza place do you think the zookeeper goes most often?

   a. Cheesy Delite

   b. Mama Mia's

   c. Piece o' Pizza

10. Which street has the most purple houses?

   a. Anchovy Avenue

   b. Tomato Street

   c. Pepperoni Place

Sometimes an article gives you a lot of information. To keep track of it all, look for the main ideas and the details. Then write them down. Here's how.

READ this article.

Topic: Fan Worship

When it comes to sports and music, people go a little crazy. For instance, fans of Wisconsin's Green Bay Packers football team have sold out every home game since 1960. They're known as "cheeseheads" because they wear foam cheese hats on their heads. Some of the male fans even go shirtless to games in the middle of winter!

Rock music has big fans too. The early 1960s were famous for "Beatlemania," where crowds of fans screamed so loud at Beatles concerts that no one could hear the music. Later fans of the Grateful Dead (called "Dead Heads") followed their favorite band all over the country. Two famous Dead Heads are ice cream makers Ben & Jerry, who named the flavor "Cherry Garcia" after Jerry Garcia, the lead singer of the Grateful Dead.

FILL IN the main ideas and details.

Main Idea 1

_____

Details

1. _____

2. _____

Main Idea 2

_____

Details

1. _____

2. _____

Check It!

Page 29

Main idea 1: Sports

Details
1. Cheesehead Packer fans
2. Shirtless male fans in winter

Main idea 2: Music

Details
1. Beatlemania screaming fans
2. Dead Heads

Page 31

Main Idea 1: Bigfoot

Details:
1. has many names
2. really tall
3. covered in dark hair
4. face like gorilla
5. mascot of the 2010 Olympics
6. no proof

Main Idea 2: Loch Ness Monster

Details:
1. like a dragon or dinosaur
2. protected by the Scottish government
3. no proof

Main Idea 3: Jackalope

Details
1. jackrabbit with antlers
2. milk can cure sickness
3. imitates human voice
4. might be caused by virus in real rabbits

READ the article.

Topic: Cryptids

Believe it or not, there's a word for the study of legendary creatures: *cryptozoology*. Monsters like Bigfoot and the Loch Ness Monster fall into this category. They are *cryptids*. But is there any proof that they exist?

Our hairy friend Bigfoot is known as *Sasquatch* in North America, *Yeren* in China, and *Yowie* in Australia. He really gets around! You'd recognize him right away. He's really tall (about 7 to 10 feet) and covered in dark hair, with a face like a gorilla. There's no concrete proof that he's real, but "Quatchi" is an official mascot of the 2010 Olympic Games in Vancouver.

Down in the dark depths of a lake in Scotland you'll find "Nessie," the Loch Ness Monster. She's been described as a creature like a dragon or a dinosaur. In spite of some photographs, movies, and sonar tests, no one can really prove she exists. But if she does, she'll be safe. Nessie's officially recognized by the Scottish government, and no one is allowed to hurt her.

Then there's the Jackalope—a jackrabbit with big antlers like an antelope. Legend says milk from a jackalope can cure sickness and that Jackalopes can imitate the human voice. However, experts believe that jackalopes really *do* exist, sort of. Rabbits can get a virus that gives them big, hornlike growths on their heads. From far away, these sick rabbits look just like Jackalopes!

FILL IN the main ideas and details.

Main Idea 1

_____

Details

1. _____

2. _____

3. _____

4. _____

5. _____

6. _____

Main Idea 2

_____

Details

1. _____

2. _____

3. _____

Main Idea 3

_____

Details

1. _____

2. _____

3. _____

4. _____

Main Idea & Details

PICK a new nonfiction article or book to read today. As you read, LOOK FOR the main ideas and details, and WRITE them on this sheet.

Main ideas	Details

You know you've really read something when you can answer questions about it. Let's look at two kinds of questions: **Right There** and **Think & Search**.

READ this article.

> ### Long Live the Queen!
>
> Elizabeth II was only 25 when she became Queen of England after the death of her father, King George VI. She was crowned in 1952. Next in line for the throne is the Queen's son, Prince Charles. But since the Queen's mother (also a Queen Elizabeth) lived to be 101, Elizabeth II may reign for many more years!

The answer to a **Right There** question can be found in one sentence (or word).

1. How old was Elizabeth II when she became Queen?

_____

See? The answer is "Right There!"

You'll find the answer to a **Think & Search** question in more than one place.

2. Who were Queen Elizabeth's parents?

_____

_____

You had to look around for that one, right?

Keep going. You'll never be afraid of a pop quiz again!

Check It!

Page 33

1. 25
2. King George VI and Queen Elizabeth

Page 34

1. A: Yes.
2. A: Rodeo cowboys
3. B: Buster Keaton, Harold Lloyd, Helen Holmes, and Jackie Chan
4. B: pratfalls, horse riding, jumping onto a moving train, leaping off a building

Page 35

1. A: Hula Hoop
2. B: swallowing goldfish, flagpole sitting, Pet Rocks, Cabbage Patch dolls
3. Suggested Q: How many people watched a man sit on a flagpole in 1929?
4. Suggested A: 20,000

Page 36

Suggestions.
1. Q: How old was Iggy when his strength was discovered?
   A: Three years old

2. Q: What can Iggy do because he's so strong?
   A: He throws a ball into the next town, crushes the checkers, cracks the house, and throws babysitters onto the roof.

READ the story, then ANSWER the questions.

Fall Guys and Fall Gals

Without stuntmen and women, action movies would be pretty boring. In the early days of film, actors like Buster Keaton and Harold Lloyd did their own silly pratfalls for their famous comedies. Makers of old western movies used rodeo cowboys as stuntmen because they knew how to ride (and fall off) horses. And it wasn't just men. In the silent movie series *The Hazards of Helen*, Helen Holmes jumped onto a moving train and leaped off a building! Nowadays trained professionals do the stunts for most actors, except when it's a Jackie Chan movie! This martial arts wizard always fights his own battles. He's got the broken bones to prove it!

A = Right There Question   *B = Think & Search Question*

MARK each question with an A or a B in the box. Then ANSWER the questions.

1. [ ] Do women do stunts?

_____

2. [ ] Who were some of the first stuntmen for westerns?

_____

3. [ ] Who are some actors that did their own stunts?

_____

4. [ ] What kinds of stunts were done in early movies?

_____

READ the story, then ANSWER the questions.

Just a Fad

The twentieth century was known for a lot of crazy fads. A fad is something that everybody wants to do or watch—for a short while. It's also called a *craze*, and they can be pretty crazy! Take swallowing goldfish, for example. In the 1940s, college students competed to see how many little flippers they could scarf down. Think that's weird? In 1929, 20,000 people watched a man sit on a flagpole for 49 days! The Hula Hoop was the famous fad toy of the 1950s. Cabbage Patch dolls ruled the 1980s. Pet Rocks were a huge fad toy in the 1970s. Can you think of any fads that happened during *your* lifetime?

A = Right There Question   *B = Think & Search Question*

MARK each question with an A or a B in the box. Then ANSWER the questions.

1. ☐ What was the toy fad of the 1950s?

_____

2. ☐ What crazy toys became fads in the twentieth century?

_____

Now, FILL IN this blank with one more **Right There** question:

3. _____

What's the answer?

4. _____

READ the story, then ANSWER the questions.

The Strongest Kid in the World

When my little brother Ignacio was three years old, he picked up the family SUV and held it in the air for a full minute. That's when we knew he was the strongest kid in the world. It's tricky living with him. Iggy likes to play ball, but sometimes he throws the ball into the next town! If you try to play checkers with him, he accidentally crushes the pieces in his hands. And when he gets mad—watch out! One time, Iggy kicked the floor so hard, it cracked our house down the middle. Any time he gets mad at a babysitter he tosses her onto the roof, and we have to call the fire department to get her down. More than any other kid, Iggy needs to learn how to play nice!

1. What's a **Right There** question you could ask about Iggy?

_____

What's the answer?

_____

2. What's a **Think & Search** question you could ask about Iggy?

_____

What's the answer?

_____

8

You've got **Right There** and **Think and Search** questions all figured out. Now it's time to tackle two more kinds of questions: **On Your Own** and **Author and Me**.

READ this story.

Worst Birthday Ever?

What a rotten birthday! All of Eli's friends had something else to do today—something secret. Even his parents had gone out! There were no plans for a special dinner or a cake. Worst of all, Eli's mom told him to take his little sister to the bowling alley for the afternoon. The whole way there, she kept giggling and saying: "I know something you don't know."

Eli sighed as he opened the door to the bowling alley.

Only YOU can answer an **On Your Own** question.

1. How would you feel if your birthday started out like this?

Anytime a question asks for your thoughts or imagination, you need to answer the question **On Your Own**.

You need to read between the lines to answer an **Author and Me** question.

2. What do you think will happen at the bowling alley?

The author gave you clues, and you figured out the rest!

Ready to try some more? Let's go!

✓ Check It!

Page 37

Suggestions:
1. sad, angry, lonely
2. Eli's friends and family are throwing him a surprise party.

Page 38

1. C: Chocolate bars or cocoa—which did you pick?
2. D: Because they invented the chocolate bar and eat the most chocolate.
3. Suggested Q: Do you like chocolate?
4. Suggested A: Yes!

Page 39

1. D: They're worried that the king will be killed in the joust.
2. C: Write your own opinion.
3. Suggested Q: What would happen if the king were killed?
4. Suggested A: The country would be left without a leader since there is no heir.

Page 40

1. D: A raccoon.
2. A: Keenan saw it first.
3. C: Write your own opinion.
4. B: The ghost was short, with a black mask, fluffy fur, and a long ringed tail.

READ the story, then ANSWER the questions.

A Delicious History

Chocolate has been around for 2000 years. The ancient Mayans called it *xocolatl*, which means "bitter water." For most of its history, chocolate was a drink, not a solid. It's made from the seeds of the cacao tree, found in South America. Christopher Columbus brought some cocoa seeds back with him when he returned from the New World. People in Europe fell in love with it! Chocolate drinks were expensive and mainly for the rich. Definitely for adults only! The Pilgrims thought chocolate was sinful and banned it from the Plymouth colony. Finally, a Swiss chocolate maker created a solid chocolate bar around 1875. Today the average American eats 10 to 12 pounds of chocolate a year. But in Switzerland, everybody eats about 21 pounds a year. After all, they're the chocolate experts!

C = On Your Own Question   D = Author and Me Question

MARK each question with a C or a D in the box. Then ANSWER the questions.

1. ☐ Which do you like better, chocolate bars or hot cocoa?

   _____

2. ☐ Why are Swiss people such chocolate experts?

   _____

Now, FILL IN this blank with one more **On Your Own** question:

3. _____

What's the answer?

4. _____

READ the story, then ANSWER the questions.

A Dangerous Game

Everyone except the king was nervous as the jousting began. In the first round, Sir Reginald knocked the Earl of Dorchester off his horse. Luckily the earl was all right. But in the second round, Sir Percy's lance hit Lord Cromwell right in the breastplate. Cromwell was knocked out cold with an ugly gash on his head. The king was up next. He laughed and joked as he mounted his horse. But the crowd was quiet. The king would be jousting against the Duke of Dornay. The duke didn't like to lose.

Sir Bryan Howard raced over to the duke as he got on his horse. "Listen man!" he hissed. "Remember, the king does not yet have an heir."

C = On Your Own Question   D = Author and Me Question

MARK each question with a C or a D in the box. Then ANSWER the questions.

1. ☐ Why is everyone so nervous about the joust?

   _____

2. ☐ What do you think of jousting?

   _____

Now, FILL IN this blank with one more **Author and Me** question:

3. _____

What's the answer?

4. _____

READ the story, then ANSWER the questions.

> **The Ghost of Cabin 8**
>
> Halfway through the summer, a ghost moved into Cabin 8. Keenan saw it first. He said it was short and wore a black mask. A few nights later, Oscar saw the ghost jumping off a table. It had fluffy fur and a long ringed tail. Casey didn't see it, but he heard the ghost making a high-pitched chattering sound like a monkey. The next day, all the food that they kept hidden in the cabin was torn open and eaten!
>
> "It was the ghost!" said Keenan.
>
> "Look!" cried Jeremy. "I bet it got in through that hole in the screen door."
>
> "But ghosts don't use doors," Casey pointed out.
>
> The boys didn't know what to think. Do you?

A = Right There Question   *B = Think & Search Question*

C = On Your Own Question   *D = Author and Me Question*

MARK each question with an A, B, C or D in the box. Then ANSWER the questions.

1. ☐ What was "haunting" Cabin 8?

   _____

2. ☐ Who saw the ghost first?

   _____

3. ☐ Are you afraid of ghosts?

   _____

4. ☐ What did the ghost look like?

   _____

Question Busters!

Next time you've finished reading a story or article, WRITE four questions about it. Then ANSWER your own questions. For each question, DECIDE what kind it is and WRITE an A, B, C, or D in the box.

A = Right There Question   *B = Think & Search Question*

C = On Your Own Question   *D = Author and Me Question*

The title of my reading is _____

Questions

1. ☐ _____

2. ☐ _____

3. ☐ _____

4. ☐ _____

Answers

1. _____

_____

2. _____

_____

3. _____

_____

4. _____

_____

Question Busters!

Next time you've finished reading a story or article, WRITE four questions about it. Then ANSWER your own questions. For each question, DECIDE what kind it is and WRITE an A, B, C, or D in the box.

A = Right There Question   *B = Think & Search Question*

C = On Your Own Question   *D = Author and Me Question*

The title of my reading is _____

Questions

1.
2.
3.
4.

Answers

1.

2.

3.

4.

Another great way to keep track of your facts is to COMPARE and CONTRAST. This helps you find differences between two similar subjects or similarities between two different subjects. You might even be surprised by what you find out!

FILL IN the blanks with these hockey facts.

J-shaped stick   L-shaped stick   Hit ball
Score goals   Players wear pads   Hit puck

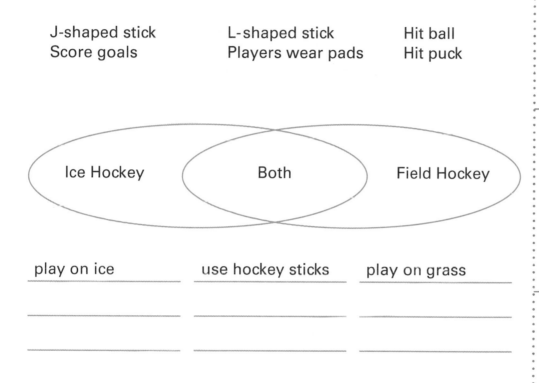

Ice Hockey   Both   Field Hockey

play on ice   use hockey sticks   play on grass

See? When you compare and contrast these two subjects, you figure out how to tell them apart, and what they have in common.

READ the paragraph, then FILL IN the blanks.

HINT: The facts are highlighted.

Storm Warning

There's a big storm rattling your windows—is it a tornado or a hurricane? Hurricanes form over the ocean, gaining power from the water, while tornados mostly form over land. Tornados are pretty skinny—they can only get as wide as 1.5 miles. But hurricanes are sometimes hundreds of miles across! A hurricane can also last for days. Tornados don't usually last for more than an hour, but they can be STRONG, with much faster winds than a hurricane. Both storms are bad news, causing floods and damage wherever they go. Hurricanes and tornados have one other thing in common: they both spin counterclockwise in the Northern Hemisphere and clockwise in the Southern Hemisphere!

Tornadoes	Both	Hurricanes

_____   _____   _____

_____   _____   _____

_____

_____

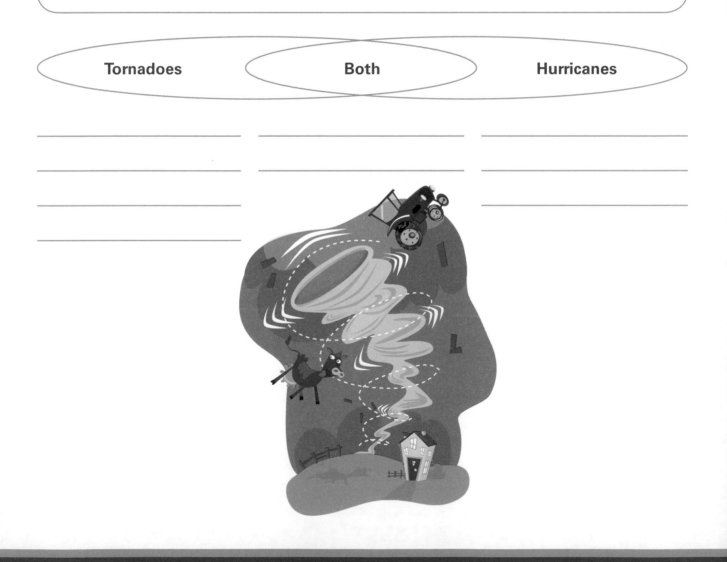

READ the paragraph, then FILL IN the blanks.

Buckle Up!

Both of my parents are safe drivers, but they've got totally different styles. Dad drives fast (sometimes a little too fast) and stops suddenly. Mom drives slow (sometimes a little too slow), and she stops gradually. In the car, they both listen to the radio, but Dad blasts rock music, while Mom listens to talk radio. Mom also likes to have the car windows open. Sometimes she leans out and yells to people she knows on the street. Ugh! Dad pumps up the AC and drums his hands on the steering wheel. They both love to drive. But Mom makes me nervous sometimes because, when she talks to me, she stops looking at the road. I always have to remind her she's driving!

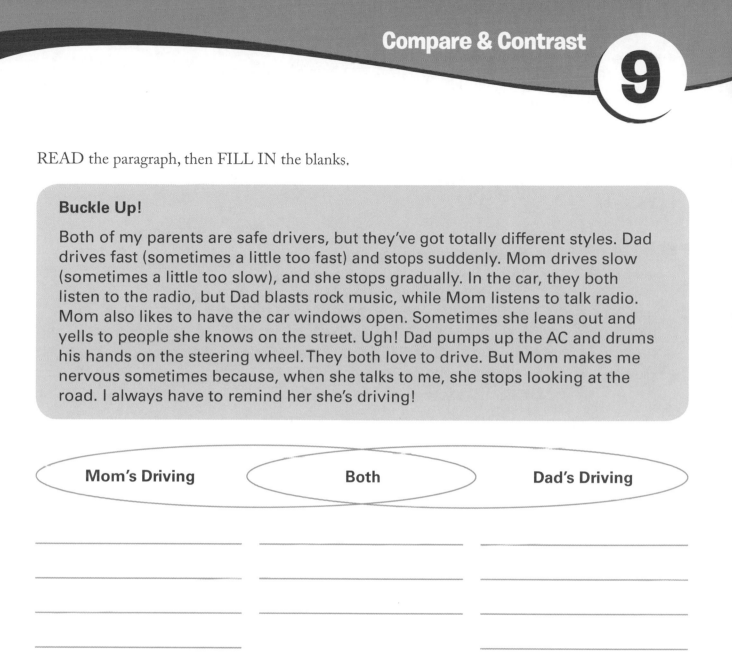

Mom's Driving   **Both**   **Dad's Driving**

READ the paragraph, then FILL IN the blanks.

Movie Night

Pietown has two movie theaters: the Royale and the MovieBox. They have six screens each. My favorite is MovieBox, but my best friend Gil says Royale is best. I don't see why! The screens at Royale are bigger, but the seats at the MovieBox are way more comfortable. And the popcorn at the MovieBox is fresh. The Royale serves stale popcorn. AND Royale doesn't have Slushies! On the other hand, the Royale does get better movies, mostly action and horror. Sometimes, the MovieBox only has boring romances or movies from other countries. And they both show too many previews!

MovieBox   **Both**   **Royale**

_____ _____ _____

_____ _____ _____

_____ _____ _____

_____

There's lots of information in fiction stories: setting, main characters, problems, solutions. To keep track of it all, make a STORY PLAN. After you've filled out a story plan, you'll have a quickie version of the story right there to help you remember everything that happened. Check it out!

FILL IN the missing information in this story plan. We've gotten you started.

Cinderella Goes to the Ball

The story takes place <u>once upon a time, in a land far, far away</u>.

1_____ is a character in the story who <u>has a mean stepmother and two ugly stepsisters</u>. 2_____

is another character in this story who has a magic wand.

The first thing that happens in the story is that <u>Cinderella finds out there's going to be a ball at the prince's castle</u>.

A problem occurs when 3_____

_____.

After that, <u>Cinderella's fairy godmother appears and offers to help but Cinderella has nothing to wear and no way to get to the ball</u>. The problem is solved when 4_____

_____.

The story ends with 5_____

_____.

Now that you're all warmed up, let's do some more!

READ the story.

The Pirates of Pieville

In the 1700s, Pieville was filled with pirates. In fact, it used to be called "Pirateville." The town was a mess! The pirates were always fighting and stealing and digging for buried treasure.

Percy the Pirate was the worst. When he was at sea, he'd shoot down any ship he saw, then kidnap the people on board. One day, he captured a sailor from Italy named Sergio Minnatti. Sergio was funny, and he played the guitar, so Percy took him back to Pirateville to be his personal musician. Sergio loved playing for the pirates! One day, Percy was really hungry after a day of digging for treasure. But when he came home, he found that his cook had been kidnapped by another pirate gang.

"WHAT!??" hollered Percy. "I need to eat!"

"I'll cook you up a lunch, don't worry," said Sergio. He rushed to the kitchen and made the only thing he really knew how to cook.

Percy looked at it with a frown. Then he sniffed it. "What's this?" he asked.

Sergio smiled nervously. "It's called *pizza*, sir. It's popular in Italy. Try it!"

So Percy tried it. He took one bite after another. Then he smiled!

"I love it! This will be the official food of Pirateville from now on!"

And that's how pizza came to Pieville.

FILL IN the missing information in this story plan.

Title: _____

The story takes place in <u>Pieville in the 1700s</u>. 1 _____

is a character in the story <u>who shoots down boats and kidnaps the sailors</u>.

2 _____ is another character in this story

who is a <u>sailor from Italy</u>. The first thing that happens in the story is that

3 _____

_____

A problem occurs when 4 _____.

The problem is solved when 5 _____.

The story ends with 6 _____.

READ the story.

Slam Dunk!

It was a hot summer day in New York City, and Graciela Cordez was stuck in her apartment. Graciela sat in the window and stared down the street.

"This stinks!" she sighed.

Then she saw a bunch of little creatures swarming through the streets from the river. Was it rats? Was it aliens?

"It's donuts!" cried Graciela.

Donuts of all kinds were rolling uphill from the donut factory. Then they attacked! Graciela watched as a hundred jelly-filled monsters swarmed over a girl on the corner and rolled her away. A giant gang of powdered donut holes surrounded the playground.

Graciela's father was a general in the army. She called him up and told him what was happening.

"Donuts, you say?" he said. "How can we fight donuts?"

"Listen!" said Graciela. "I know exactly what to do."

So an hour later, the army came. It had a big tanker truck that said "Coffee" in big green letters. The truck had a hose attached. The soldiers went down the city streets, spraying the donuts with coffee.

It worked! The donuts got dunked. Then everyone ate them.

Graciela got a medal from the President for her smart idea.

FILL IN the missing information in this story plan.

Title: _____

The story takes place 1_____.

2_____ is a character in the story who

3_____. Graciela's father is another

character in this story who 4_____.

The first thing that happens in the story is that

5_____.

A problem occurs when 6_____.

The problem is solved when 7_____.

The story ends with 8_____.

READ the story.

Down in the Basement

After her family moved in, Cassie hated the new apartment building right away.

"Where are all the kids?" she asked.

"Maybe they're at the playground," her mother said. She wanted Cassie to be happy. "Let's take a look."

But the kids in the playground were all too young.

"I guess there aren't any kids my age around here," Cassie sighed.

One day, Cassie's mother came up from the building's basement with a special smile.

"Would you like to help me wash some clothes?" she asked.

Cassie had nothing fun to do, so she went down to the laundry room with her mother. When they stepped out of the elevator into the basement, Cassie heard lots of shouting and laughter.

"What's that?" she asked.

"Why don't you check it out?" her mother said.

Cassie opened a door across from the laundry room and gasped. Inside the big room, a bunch of kids her age were playing games, jumping rope, and listening to music, while a few parents watched.

"Hi!" said a girl. "You must be the new kid. Want to pretend to be princesses locked in a tower?"

And that's how Cassie spent the afternoon.

FILL IN the story plan.

Title: _____

The story takes place 1_____.

2_____ is a character in the story

who 3_____.

4_____ is another character in the story

who 5_____.

The first thing that happens in the story is that 6_____

_____.

A problem occurs when 7_____

_____.

The problem is solved when 8_____

_____.

The story ends with 9_____

_____.

Compare & Contrast

PICK an article or story to read, and CHOOSE two subjects to compare and contrast. Then FILL OUT this worksheet.

The title is _____

I'm comparing and contrasting

subject 1, _____

with subject 2, _____

Details about subject 1

1. _____

2. _____

3. _____

4. _____

5. _____

Details about subject 2

1. _____

2. _____

3. _____

4. _____

5. _____

For each detail ask yourself, is this detail something that belongs to only one of the subjects, or is it really something that is shared by both?

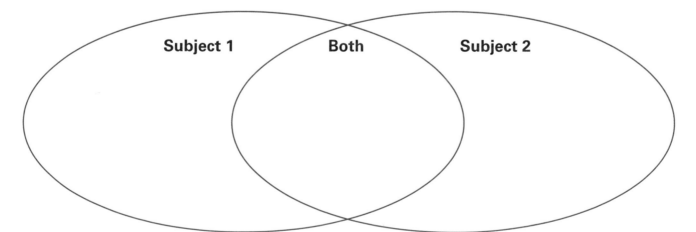

Subject 1   **Both**   **Subject 2**

Story Plan

PICK a story you've already read, then FILL OUT this worksheet.

Title _____

Main character _____

Character details _____

The setting _____

The first thing that happens is _____

_____

The problem _____

After that _____

After that _____

The solution _____

_____

_____

Story Plan

PICK a story you've already read, then FILL OUT this worksheet.

Title _____

Main character _____

Character details _____

The setting _____

The first thing that happens is _____

_____

The problem _____

After that _____

After that _____

The solution _____

_____

_____

Section 2:
Summer Smart Math

1

Secret Number

DRAW a line to get from the start of the maze to the end without taking any extra paths. WRITE each number you cross in order, starting with the millions place, to find the secret number.

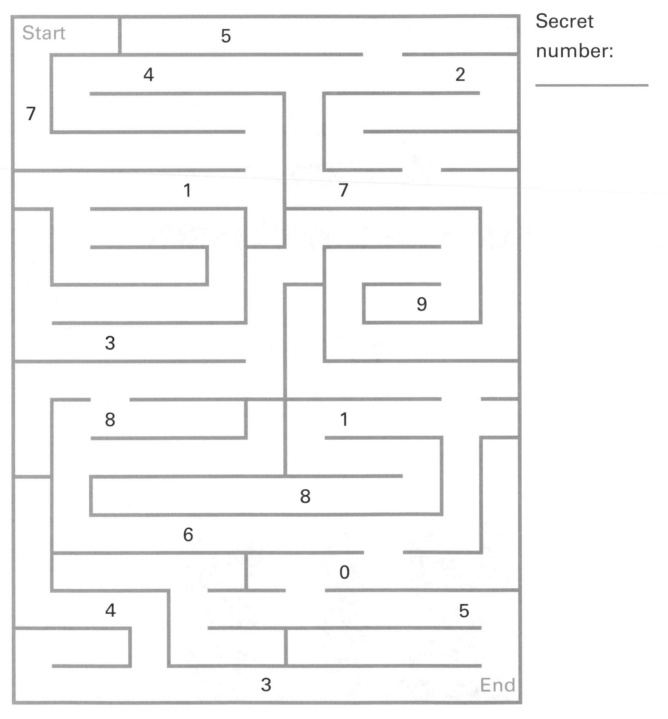

Secret
number:

_____

Number Search

WRITE each number. Then CIRCLE it in the puzzle.

HINT: Numbers are across and down only.

1. eighty-four thousand, one hundred sixty-five 84,165

2. four million, six hundred seventy-two thousand, two hundred forty-four _____

3. nine hundred sixty-one thousand, seven hundred twenty-three _____

4. twenty-nine thousand, eight hundred eleven _____

5. one hundred fifteen thousand, seven hundred thirty-six _____

6. two million, eighty-two thousand, six hundred forty-one _____

7. five hundred five thousand, six hundred ninety-two _____

8. three million, nine hundred thirty-seven thousand, two hundred sixty _____

2	9	8	1	1	0	0	2
9	5	0	5	6	9	2	0
8	1	8	2	4	6	7	8
2	4	4	9	9	1	3	2
0	5	1	1	5	7	3	6
3	4	6	7	2	2	4	4
6	0	5	3	7	3	4	1
3	9	3	7	2	6	0	8

② Just Right

WRITE each of the numbers to correctly complete the sentences.

HINT: There may be more than one place to put a number, but you need to use every number.

| 341,156 | 392,382 | 275,319 | 337,236 | 232,981 |
| 384,620 | 228,864 | 382,495 | 246,518 | |

1. _____ rounded to the nearest thousand is 229,000.

2. _____ rounded to the nearest ten thousand is 340,000.

3. _____ rounded to the nearest hundred thousand is 300,000.

4. _____ rounded to the nearest ten thousand is 380,000.

5. _____ rounded to the nearest thousand is 382,000.

6. _____ rounded to the nearest hundred thousand is 400,000.

7. _____ rounded to the nearest ten thousand is 230,000.

8. _____ rounded to the nearest thousand is 337,000.

9. _____ rounded to the nearest hundred thousand is 200,000.

Picking Pairs

DRAW a line to connect each number with that number rounded to the nearest hundred thousand.

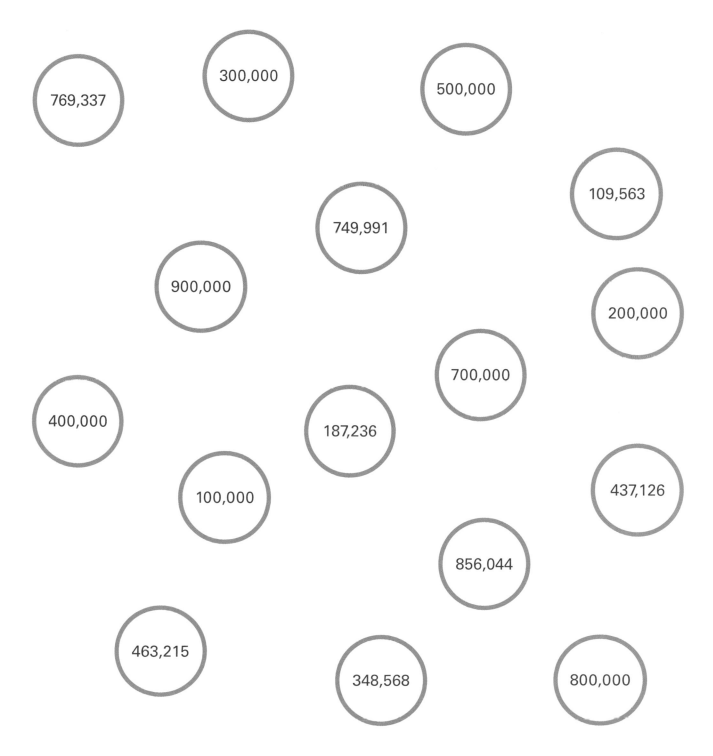

2 Just Right

WRITE each of the numbers to correctly complete the sentence.

HINT: There may be more than one place to put a number, but you need to use every number.

| 5,418,163 | 5,908,752 | 5,826,138 | 6,692,556 | 5,237,564 |
| 6,694,204 | 5,879,215 | 5,418,921 | 6,563,827 | |

1. _____ rounded to the nearest million is 5,000,000.

2. _____ rounded to the nearest hundred thousand is 5,400,000.

3. _____ rounded to the nearest ten thousand is 5,910,000.

4. _____ rounded to the nearest hundred thousand is 6,700,000.

5. _____ rounded to the nearest thousand is 6,694,000.

6. _____ rounded to the nearest million is 7,000,000.

7. _____ rounded to the nearest hundred thousand is 5,900,000.

8. _____ rounded to the nearest thousand is 5,419,000.

9. _____ rounded to the nearest million is 6,000,000.

Number Factory

WRITE the numbers that belong on the side of each machine.

HINT: The numbers are all between 1 and 10.

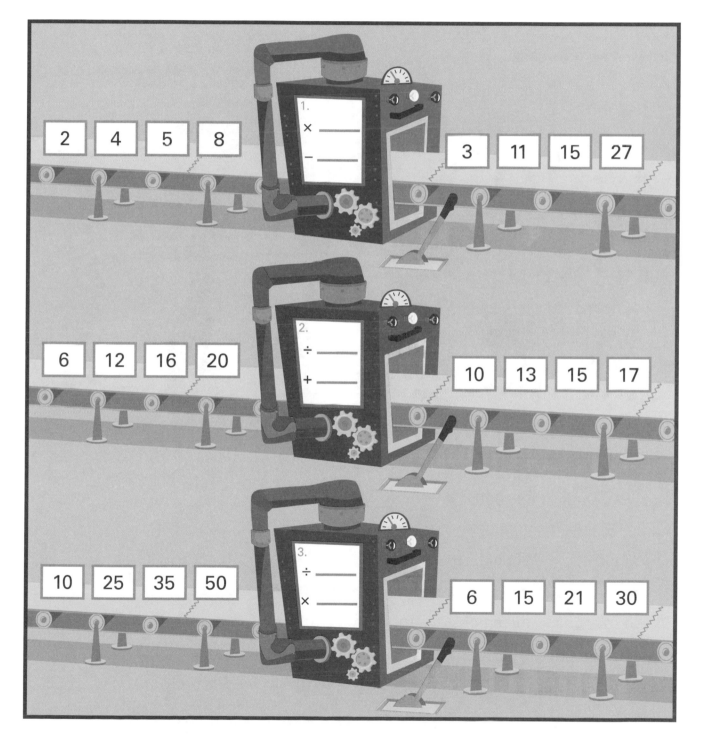

Who Am I?

READ the clues, and CIRCLE the mystery number.

HINT: Cross out any number that does not match the clues.

I am more than 1,500,000.

I am less than 2,500,000.

I have a 1 in the millions place.

When rounded to the nearest hundred thousand, I'm 1,800,000.

When rounded to the nearest ten thousand, I'm 1,840,000.

Who am I?

Pipe Down

WRITE the missing number. Then FOLLOW the pipe, and WRITE the same number in the next problem.

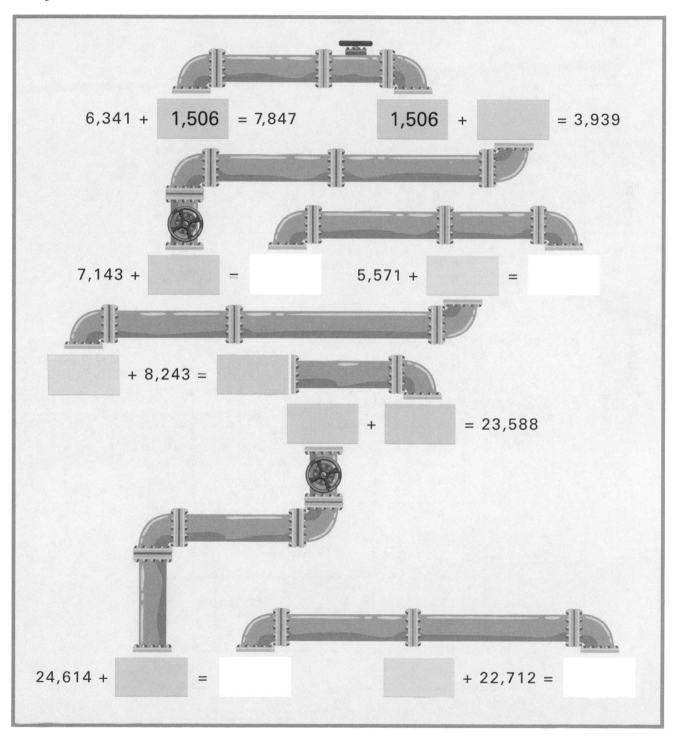

6,341 + **1,506** = 7,847   **1,506** + ⬜ = 3,939

7,143 + ⬜ = ⬜   5,571 + ⬜ = ⬜

⬜ + 8,243 = ⬜

⬜ + ⬜ = 23,588

24,614 + ⬜ = ⬜   ⬜ + 22,712 = ⬜

4

Number Search

WRITE each sum. Then CIRCLE it in the puzzle.

HINT: Numbers are across and down only.

1. 48,350
    + 28,627

2. 16,129
    + 69,414

3. 39,524
    + 11,825

4. 36,942
    + 22,926

5. 85,924
    + 13,834

6. 46,561
    + 15,811

7. 21,842
    + 18,861

8. 43,527
    + 27,703

4	0	7	0	3	6	5	7
1	3	9	8	5	2	2	6
0	9	9	5	1	3	4	9
8	6	7	0	4	7	9	7
5	4	5	7	9	2	0	7
5	9	8	6	8	3	1	5
4	9	2	7	1	2	3	0
3	1	1	4	0	8	7	4

Pipe Down

WRITE the missing number. Then FOLLOW the pipe, and WRITE the same number in the next problem.

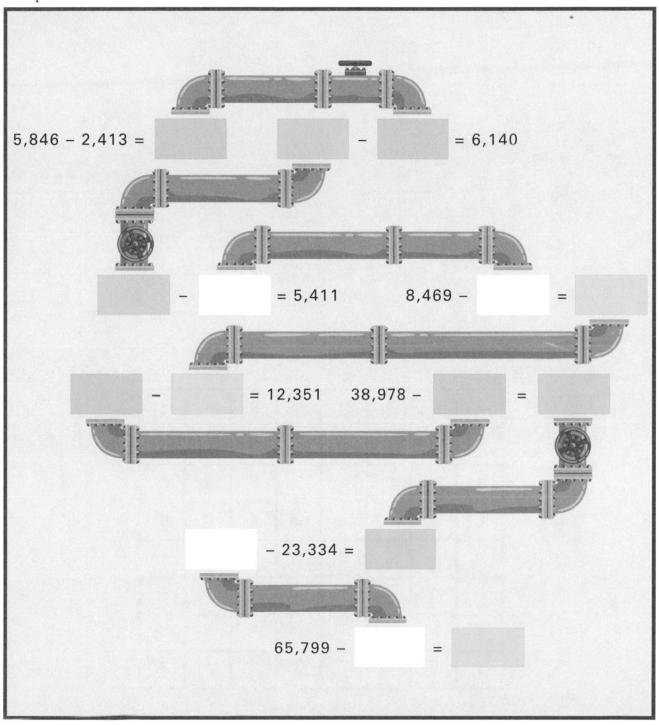

5,846 − 2,413 = [____]   [____] − [____] = 6,140

[____] − [____] = 5,411   8,469 − [____] = [____]

[____] − [____] = 12,351   38,978 − [____] = [____]

[____] − 23,334 = [____]

65,799 − [____] = [____]

Number Search

WRITE each difference. Then CIRCLE it in the puzzle.

HINT: Numbers are across and down only.

1. 50,308
    − 27,997

2. 94,690
    − 18,477

3. 83,818
    − 28,594

4. 90,620
    − 19,602

5. 69,262
    − 19,386

6. 54,532
    − 36,296

7. 87,855
    − 26,769

8. 45,199
    − 10,227

1	8	2	3	6	9	6	1
7	6	2	4	6	0	1	7
1	1	0	2	3	5	0	1
3	5	5	2	2	4	8	0
4	2	2	3	5	9	6	1
9	0	4	1	6	8	1	8
7	6	2	1	3	7	6	2
2	9	8	8	3	6	7	2

Picking Pairs

ESTIMATE each sum or difference by rounding to the nearest ten thousand. DRAW a line to connect each problem with the correct estimate of the sum or difference.

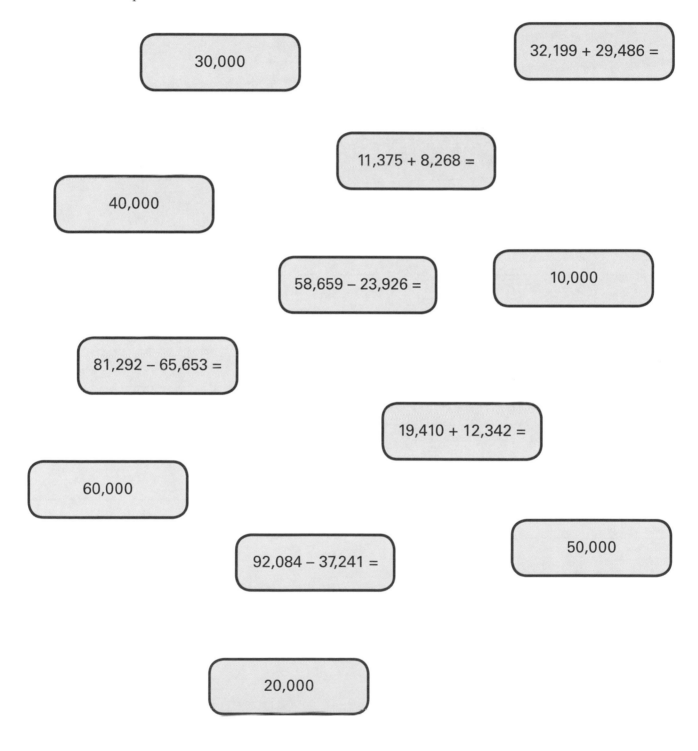

30,000

32,199 + 29,486 =

11,375 + 8,268 =

40,000

58,659 − 23,926 =

10,000

81,292 − 65,653 =

19,410 + 12,342 =

60,000

92,084 − 37,241 =

50,000

20,000

Hidden Design

ESTIMATE each sum or difference by rounding each number to the nearest thousand. Then COLOR the squares that match the numbers to see the hidden design.

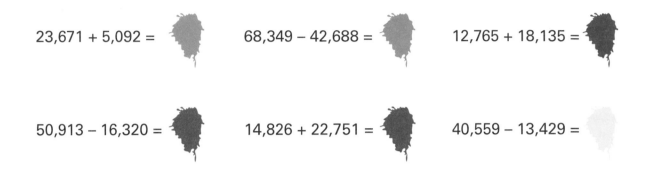

23,671 + 5,092 =

68,349 − 42,688 =

12,765 + 18,135 =

50,913 − 16,320 =

14,826 + 22,751 =

40,559 − 13,429 =

25,000	38,000	25,000	28,000	29,000	31,000	29,000	28,000
38,000	35,000	38,000	25,000	28,000	29,000	28,000	25,000
35,000	31,000	35,000	38,000	25,000	28,000	25,000	38,000
31,000	29,000	31,000	35,000	38,000	25,000	38,000	35,000
29,000	28,000	29,000	31,000	35,000	38,000	35,000	31,000
28,000	25,000	28,000	29,000	31,000	35,000	31,000	29,000
25,000	38,000	25,000	28,000	29,000	31,000	29,000	28,000
38,000	35,000	38,000	25,000	28,000	29,000	28,000	25,000

Code Breaker

SOLVE each problem. WRITE the letter that matches each product to solve the riddle.

6 × 5	8 × 2	9 × 4	5 × 5	3 × 8	10 × 6
1	2	3	4	5	6
M	R	W	U	V	H

7 × 1	9 × 8	6 × 8	2 × 9	9 × 5	10 × 4
7	8	9	10	11	12
Y	E	P	T	O	I

Where do you find a turtle with no legs?

__ __ __ __ __ __ __ __
36 60 72 16 72 24 72 16

__ __ __ __ __ __ __ __ __ .
7 45 25 48 25 18 60 40 30

Gridlock

WRITE numbers so that the product of the rows and columns is correct.

HINT: Use only the numbers 1 through 10.

Example:

	3	5
4	12	20
8	24	40

$3 \times 4 = 12$

$3 \times 8 = 24$

$5 \times 4 = 20$

$5 \times 8 = 40$

	4	7
	8	14

	5	6
	15	18

	18	63
	20	70

	10	16
	30	48

	21	56
	27	72

	35	42
	45	54

Pipe Down

WRITE the missing number. Then FOLLOW the pipe, and WRITE the same number in the next problem.

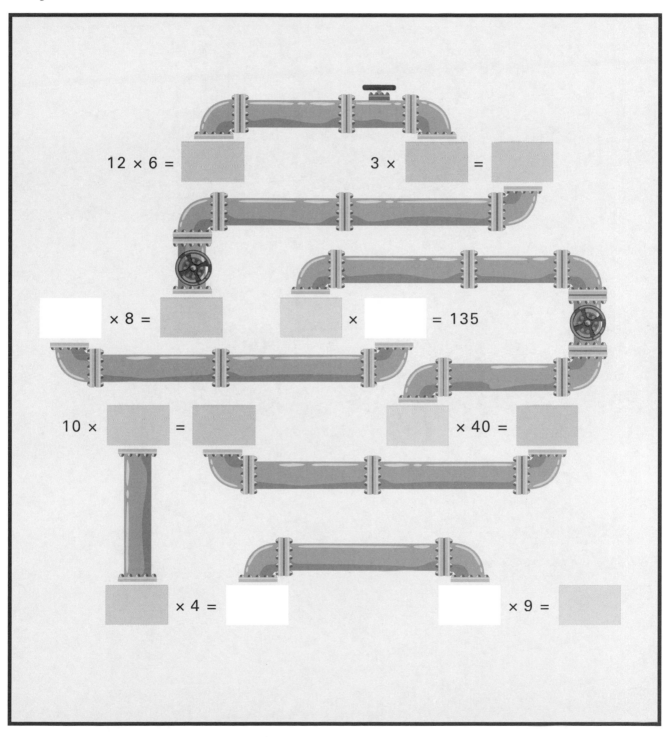

12 × 6 = ☐   3 × ☐ = ☐

☐ × 8 = ☐   ☐ × ☐ = 135

10 × ☐ = ☐   ☐ × 40 = ☐

☐ × 4 = ☐   ☐ × 9 = ☐

Super Square

WRITE numbers in the empty squares to finish all of the multiplication problems.

13	×	11	=	
×		×		×
6	×		=	
=		=		=
	×	154	=	

Code Breaker

SOLVE each problem. WRITE the letter that matches each quotient to solve the riddle.

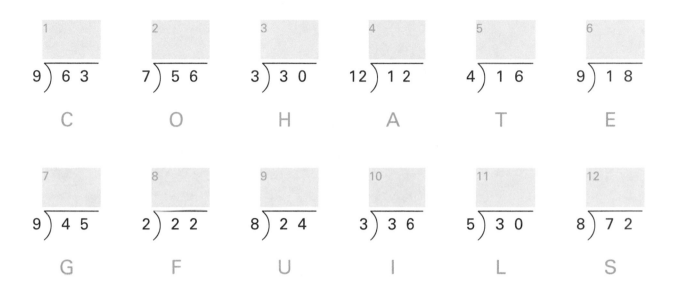

1. $9\overline{)63}$	2. $7\overline{)56}$	3. $3\overline{)30}$	4. $12\overline{)12}$	5. $4\overline{)16}$	6. $9\overline{)18}$
C	O	H	A	T	E

7. $9\overline{)45}$	8. $2\overline{)22}$	9. $8\overline{)24}$	10. $3\overline{)36}$	11. $5\overline{)30}$	12. $8\overline{)72}$
G	F	U	I	L	S

How did the frog make the baseball team?

___ ___
10   2

___ ___ ___ ___ ___ ___
7   1   3   5   10   4

___ ___ ___ ___
1   6   8   4

___ ___ ___ ___ ___ ___ ___ .
8   11   11   6   12   2   9

9

Number Factory

WRITE the numbers that will come out of each machine.

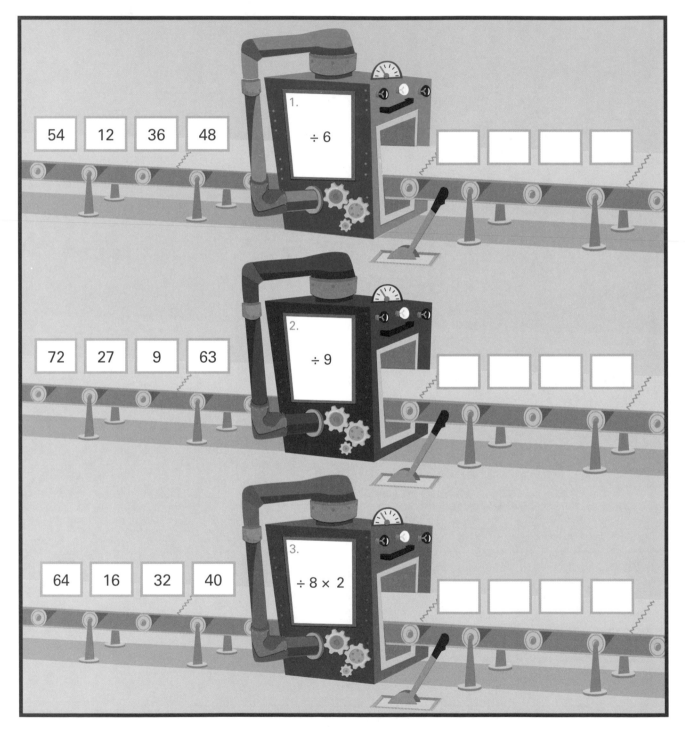

Pipe Down

WRITE the missing number. Then FOLLOW the pipe, and WRITE the same number in the next problem.

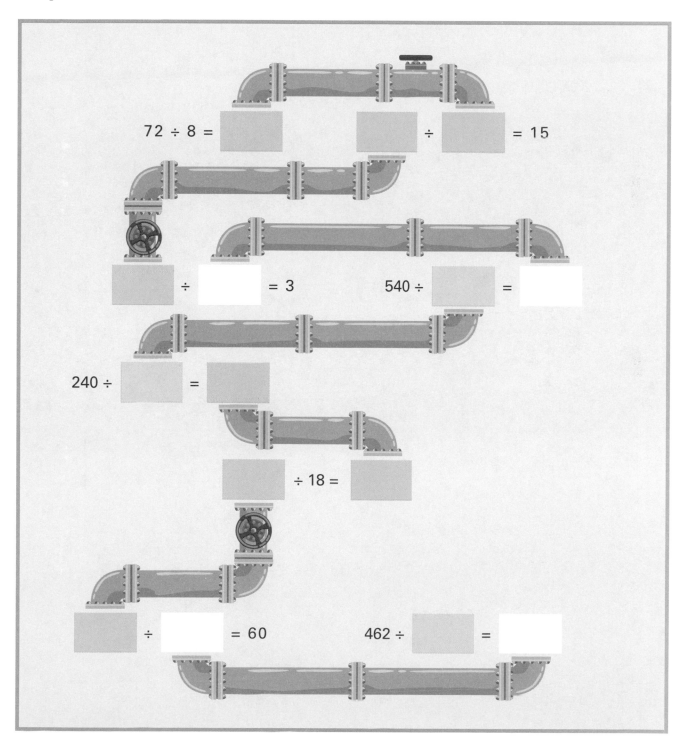

72 ÷ 8 = ___   ___ ÷ ___ = 15

___ ÷ ___ = 3   540 ÷ ___ = ___

240 ÷ ___ = ___

___ ÷ 18 = ___

___ ÷ ___ = 60   462 ÷ ___ = ___

10

Super Square

WRITE numbers in the empty squares to finish all of the division problems.

972	÷	36	=	
÷		÷		÷
54	÷		=	
=		=		=
	÷	6	=	

What's the Password?

WRITE the letters that form a fraction of each word. Then WRITE the letters in order to find the secret password.

1. The first $\frac{1}{3}$ of **SURVEY**   _____

2. The first $\frac{1}{7}$ of **MISSING**   _____

3. The first $\frac{2}{9}$ of **MESMERIZE**   _____

4. The last $\frac{1}{6}$ of **WINTER**   _____

5. The first $\frac{3}{7}$ of **VACCINE**   _____

6. The middle $\frac{1}{5}$ of **GRAVY**   _____

7. The first $\frac{1}{2}$ of **TINY**   _____

8. The last $\frac{2}{7}$ of **HEXAGON**   _____

Password:

_____ ___ _____ _____ _____

_____ ___ ____ _____ _____

Picking Pairs

DRAW a line to connect each decimal with the correct picture.

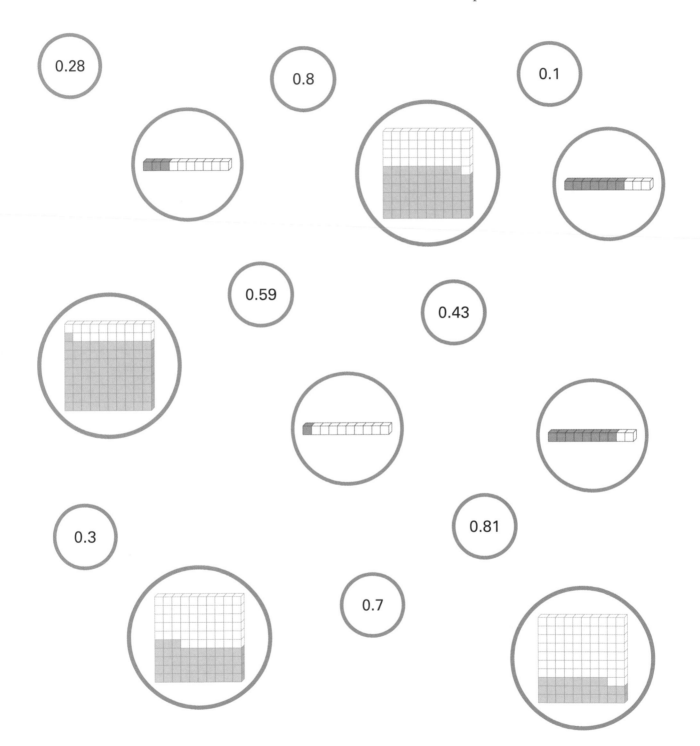

Code Breaker

SOLVE each problem. WRITE the letter that matches each sum to solve the riddle.

$\frac{1}{4} + \frac{2}{4} = $ ¹ ___ H	$\frac{1}{6} + \frac{4}{6} = $ ² ___ B	$\frac{2}{3} + \frac{1}{3} = $ ³ ___ T
$\frac{1}{9} + \frac{4}{9} = $ ⁴ ___ L	$\frac{3}{8} + \frac{4}{8} = $ ⁵ ___ E	$\frac{1}{5} + \frac{1}{5} = $ ⁶ ___ R
$\frac{1}{3} + \frac{1}{3} = $ ⁷ ___ A	$\frac{3}{7} + \frac{2}{7} = $ ⁸ ___ I	$\frac{2}{8} + \frac{3}{8} = $ ⁹ ___ Y

Which building has the most stories?

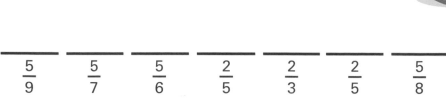

___ ___ ___
$\frac{3}{3}$ $\frac{3}{4}$ $\frac{7}{8}$

___ ___ ___ ___ ___ ___ ___ .
$\frac{5}{9}$ $\frac{5}{7}$ $\frac{5}{6}$ $\frac{2}{5}$ $\frac{2}{3}$ $\frac{2}{5}$ $\frac{5}{8}$

Number Factory

WRITE the fractions that will come out of each machine.

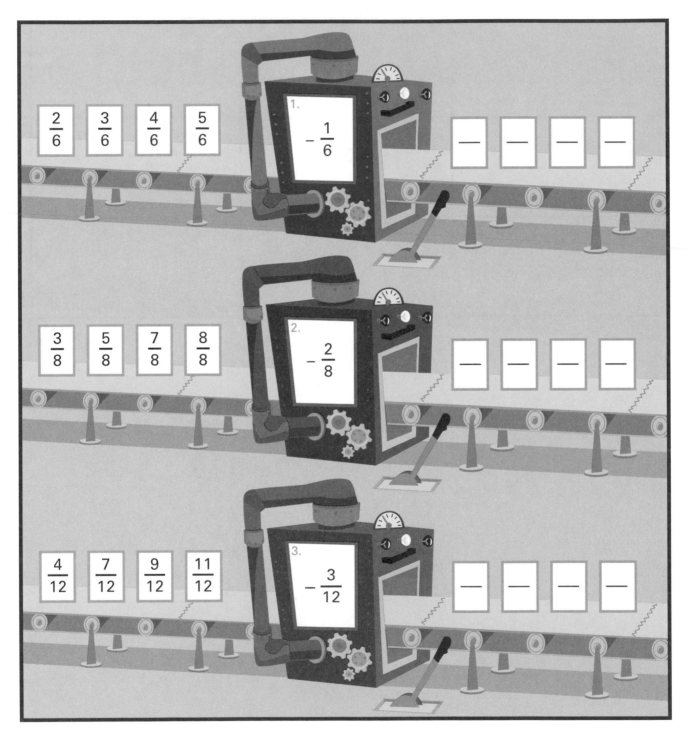

1. $-\dfrac{1}{6}$

$\dfrac{2}{6}$ $\dfrac{3}{6}$ $\dfrac{4}{6}$ $\dfrac{5}{6}$

2. $-\dfrac{2}{8}$

$\dfrac{3}{8}$ $\dfrac{5}{8}$ $\dfrac{7}{8}$ $\dfrac{8}{8}$

3. $-\dfrac{3}{12}$

$\dfrac{4}{12}$ $\dfrac{7}{12}$ $\dfrac{9}{12}$ $\dfrac{11}{12}$

Pipe Down

WRITE the missing number. Then FOLLOW the pipe, and WRITE the same number in the next problem.

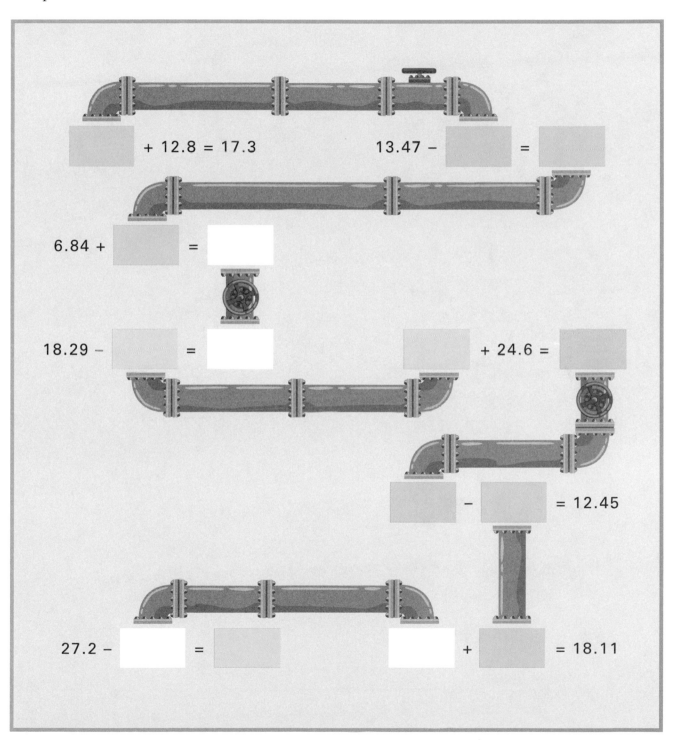

+ 12.8 = 17.3   13.47 – ⬚ =

6.84 + ⬚ =

18.29 – ⬚ =   + 24.6 =

– ⬚ = 12.45

27.2 – ⬚ =   + ⬚ = 18.11

Crossing Paths

WRITE the missing numbers.

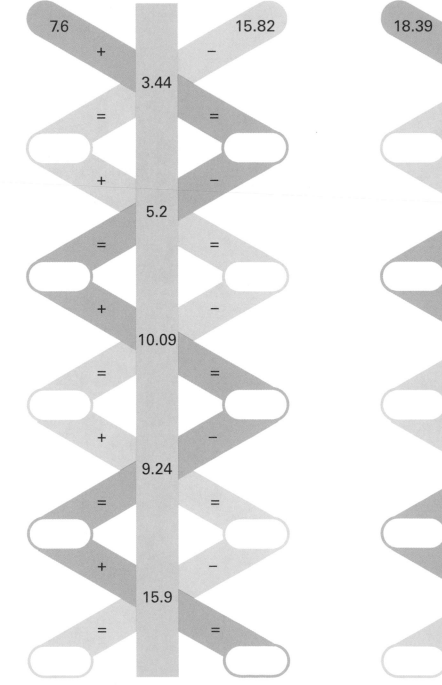

7.6   15.82

\+   −

3.44

=   =

( )   ( )

\+   −

5.2

=   =

( )   ( )

\+   −

10.09

=   =

( )   ( )

\+   −

9.24

=   =

( )   ( )

\+   −

15.9

=   =

( )   ( )

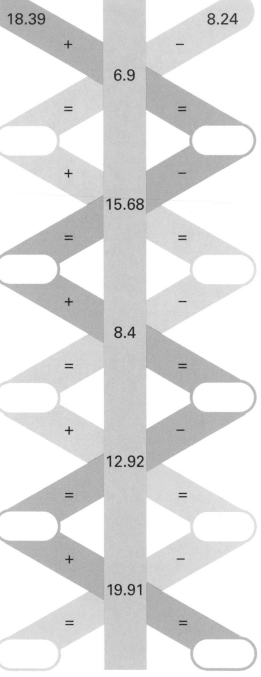

18.39   8.24

\+   −

6.9

=   =

( )   ( )

\+   −

15.68

=   =

( )   ( )

\+   −

8.4

=   =

( )   ( )

\+   −

12.92

=   =

( )   ( )

\+   −

19.91

=   =

( )   ( )

Code Ruler

WRITE the letter that matches each measurement to answer the riddle.

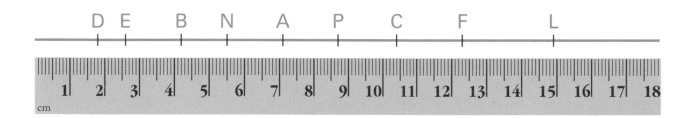

D E   B   N   A   P   C   F   L

What runs around the yard without moving?

_____   _____ _____ _____ _____ _____ .
7.1 cm   12.3 cm 2.6 cm   5.5 cm 10.4 cm   2.6 cm

14

Totally Tangled

FIND the measurements that are connected. COLOR the smaller measurement in each pair.

1 centimeter (cm) = 10 millimeters (mm)
1 meter (m) = 100 centimeters
1 kilometer (km) = 1,000 meters

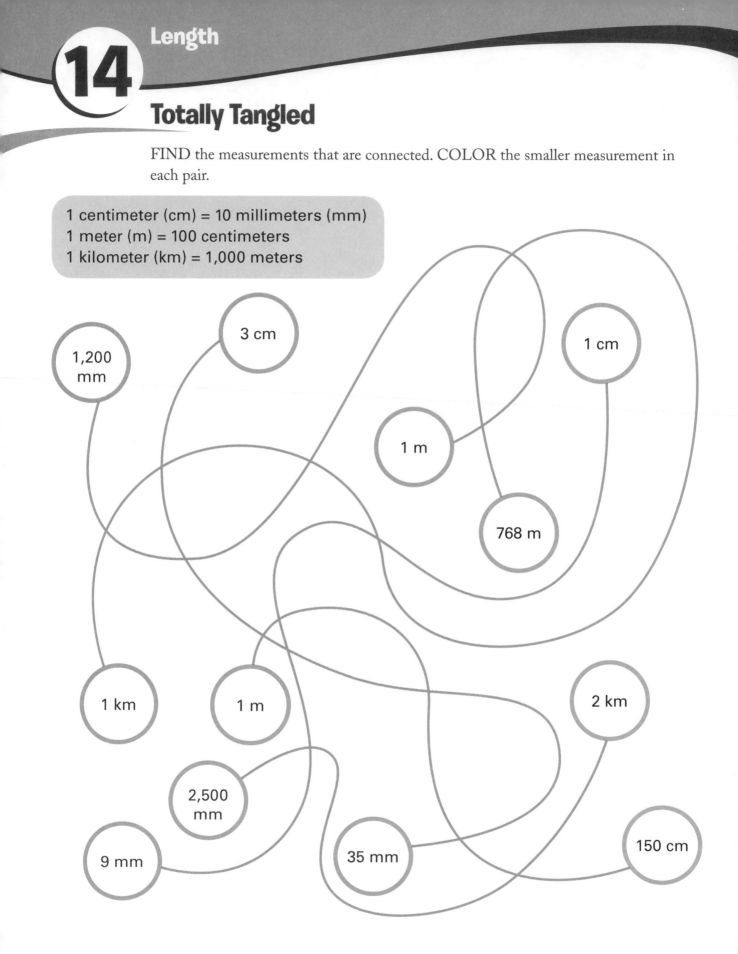

Code Ruler

WRITE the letter that matches each measurement to answer the riddle.

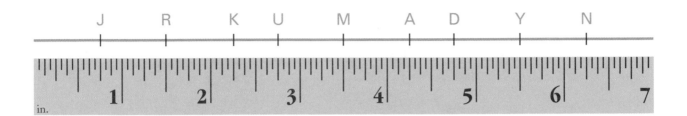

What do you call three feet of garbage?

_____ _____ _____ _____ _____ _____ _____ _____ _____ .
$4\frac{1}{4}$ in. $\frac{3}{4}$ in. $2\frac{3}{4}$ in. $6\frac{1}{4}$ in. $2\frac{1}{4}$ in. $5\frac{1}{2}$ in. $4\frac{1}{4}$ in. $1\frac{1}{2}$ in. $4\frac{3}{4}$ in.

Totally Tangled

FIND the measurements that are connected. COLOR the larger measurement in each pair.

1 foot (ft) = 12 inches (in.)
1 yard (yd) = 3 feet
1 mile (mi) = 1,760 yards or 5,280 feet

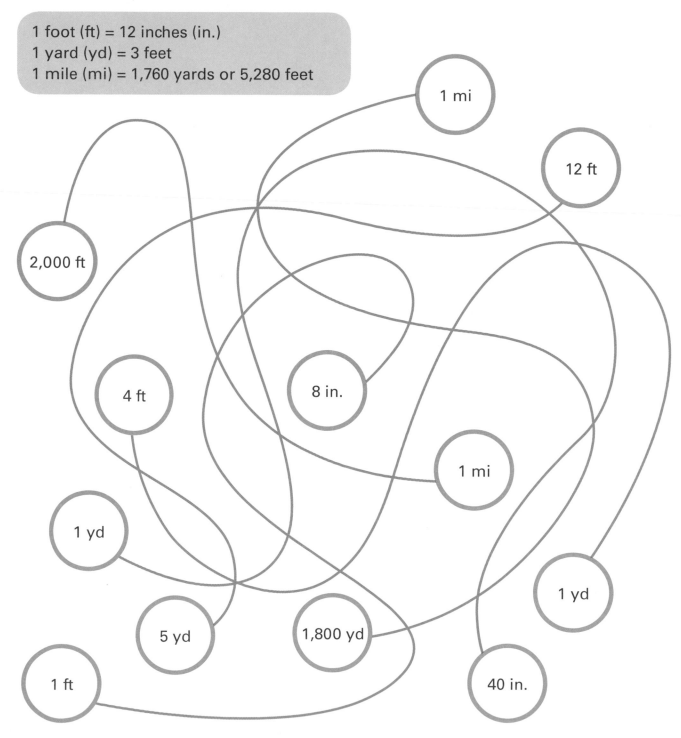

Shape Creator

DRAW three different shapes that all have a perimeter of 12 units.

Using a centimeter ruler, DRAW two different shapes with a perimeter of 20 centimeters.

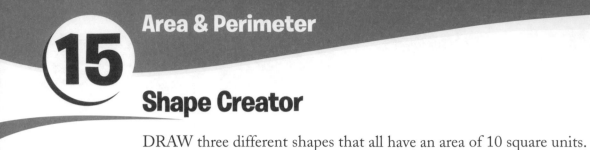

15

Shape Creator

DRAW three different shapes that all have an area of 10 square units.

Using a centimeter ruler, DRAW two different rectangles with an area of 24 square centimeters.

Code Breaker

SOLVE each problem. WRITE the letter that matches each equivalent measurement to solve the riddle.

1 gram (g) = 1,000 milligrams (mg)	1 kilogram (kg) = 1,000 grams

1 5 g = _____ mg	D	2 2,300 g = _____ kg	L
3 6 kg = _____ g	O	4 600 mg = _____ g	A
5 3,000 mg = _____ g	H	6 6.5 g = _____ mg	U
7 1.5 kg = _____ g	C	8 10,400 g = _____ kg	N
9 0.2 g = _____ mg	Y	10 1,000,000 mg = _____ kg	E

What can you add to a barrel to make it lighter?

___ ___ ___   ___ ___ ___   ___ ___ ___
200 6,000 6,500   1,500 0.6 10.4   0.6 5,000 5,000

___   ___ ___ ___ ___ .
0.6   3 6,000 2.3 1

16

Totally Tangled

FIND the measurements that are connected. COLOR the smaller measurement in each pair.

1 gram (g) = 1,000 milligrams (mg)   1 kilogram (kg) = 1,000 grams

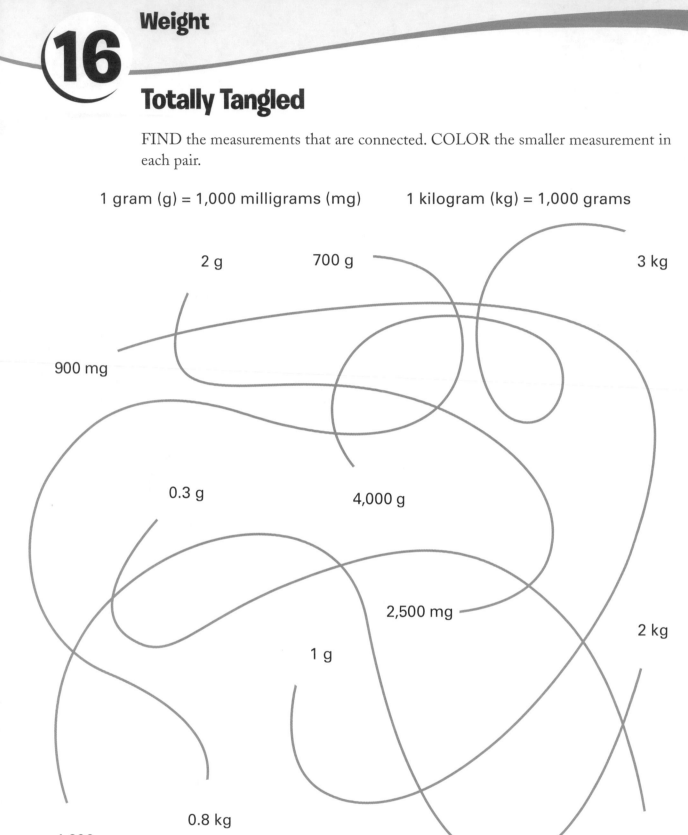

2 g   700 g   3 kg

900 mg

0.3 g   4,000 g

2,500 mg   2 kg

1 g

0.8 kg

1,900 g   400 mg

Code Breaker

SOLVE each problem. Use a fraction where necessary. WRITE the letter that matches each equivalent measurement to solve the riddle.

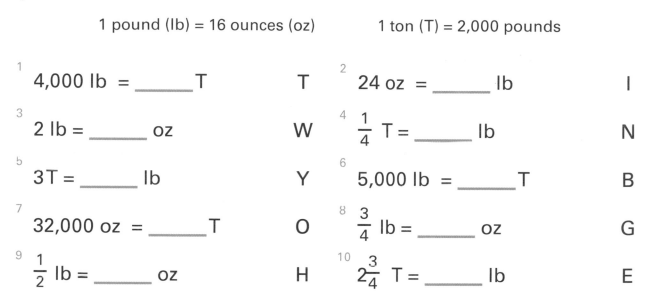

1 pound (lb) = 16 ounces (oz)   1 ton (T) = 2,000 pounds

1. 4,000 lb = _____ T   T

2. 24 oz = _____ lb   I

3. 2 lb = _____ oz   W

4. $\frac{1}{4}$ T = _____ lb   N

5. 3T = _____ lb   Y

6. 5,000 lb = _____ T   B

7. 32,000 oz = _____ T   O

8. $\frac{3}{4}$ lb = _____ oz   G

9. $\frac{1}{2}$ lb = _____ oz   H

10. $2\frac{3}{4}$ T = _____ lb   E

What weighs more, a ton of rocks or a ton of leaves?

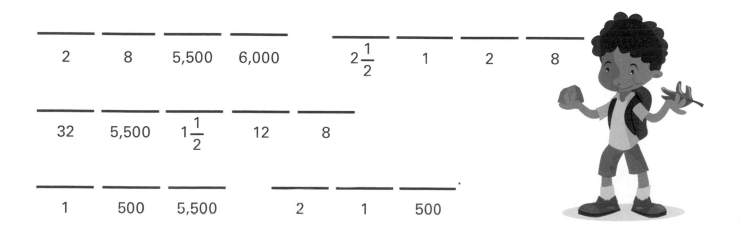

___	___	___	___		___	___	___	___
2	8	5,500	6,000		$2\frac{1}{2}$	1	2	8

___	___	___	___	___
32	5,500	$1\frac{1}{2}$	12	8

___	___	___		___	___	___
1	500	5,500		2	1	500

Totally Tangled

FIND the measurements that are connected. COLOR the larger measurement in each pair.

1 pound (lb) = 16 ounces (oz)   1 ton (T) = 2,000 pounds

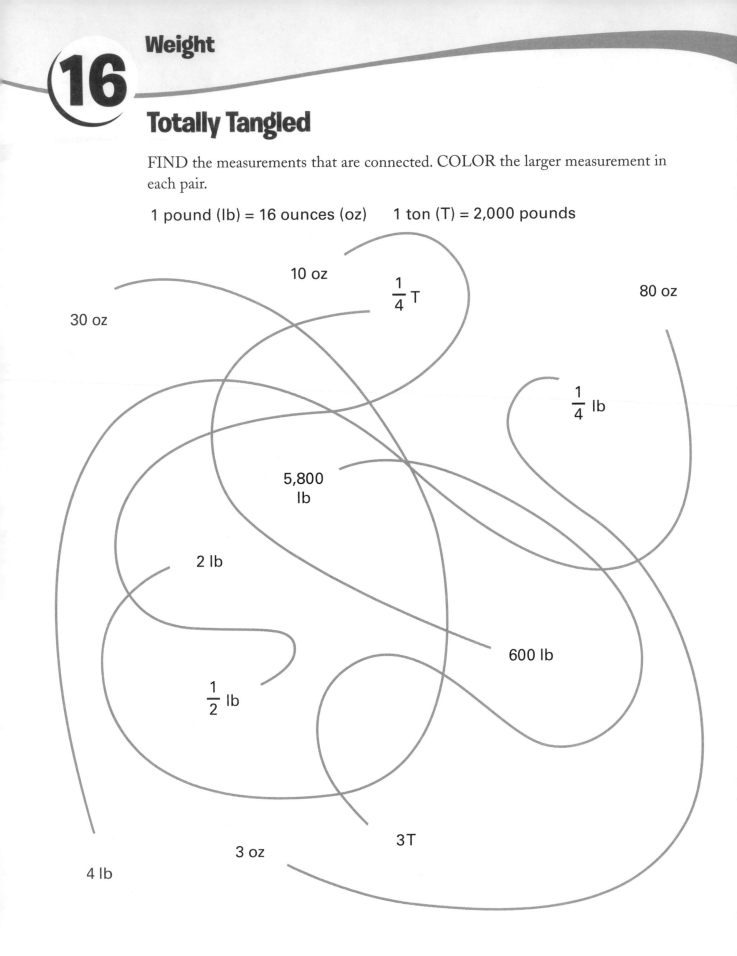

10 oz

$\frac{1}{4}$ T

80 oz

30 oz

$\frac{1}{4}$ lb

5,800 lb

2 lb

600 lb

$\frac{1}{2}$ lb

3T

3 oz

4 lb

Who Am I?

READ the clues, and CIRCLE the mystery shape.

HINT: Cross out any shape that does not match the clues.

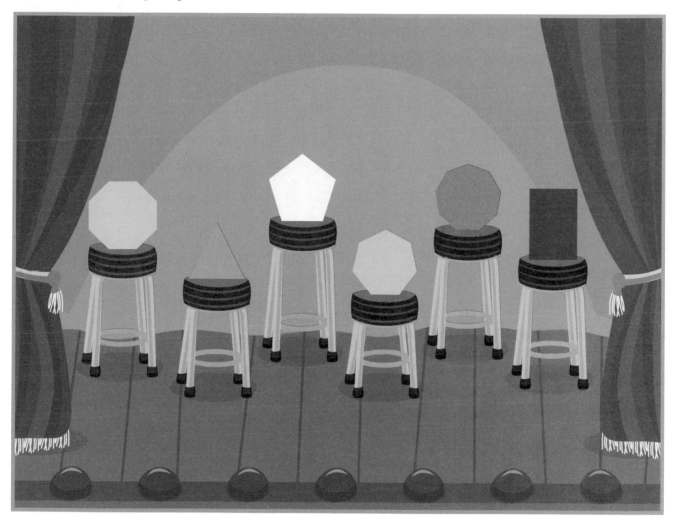

I have fewer than nine sides.

I have no acute angles.

I have more than five sides.

I have seven vertices.

Who am I?

Criss Cross

IDENTIFY each shape, and WRITE the shape names in the puzzle.

ACROSS

3.
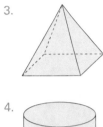

4.

5.

DOWN

1.
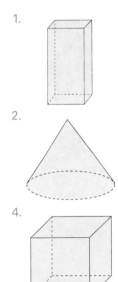

2.

4.
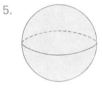

T-Shirt Shop

READ the paragraph, and WRITE the answer.

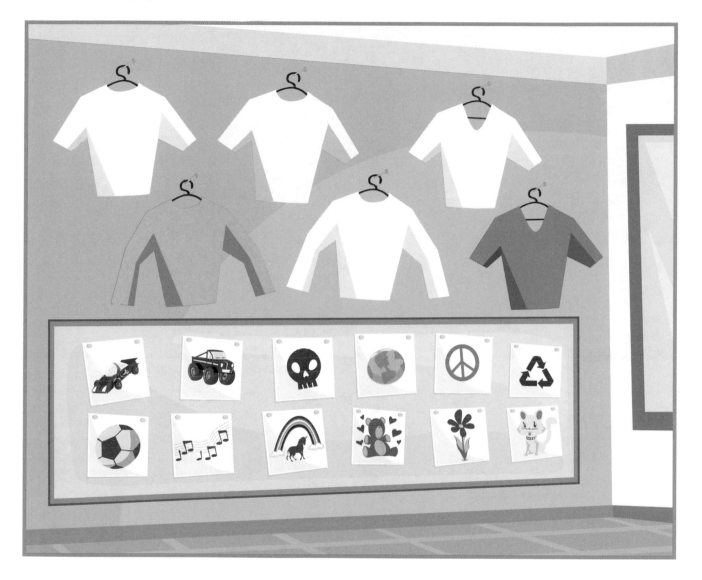

A T-shirt shop can put any design on the T-shirt of your choice. There are 6 different T-shirts and 12 different designs, and you can choose to have your name put on the back or not. How many different T-shirts can you make?

_____ T-shirts

All You Can Eat

READ the paragraph, and WRITE the answer.

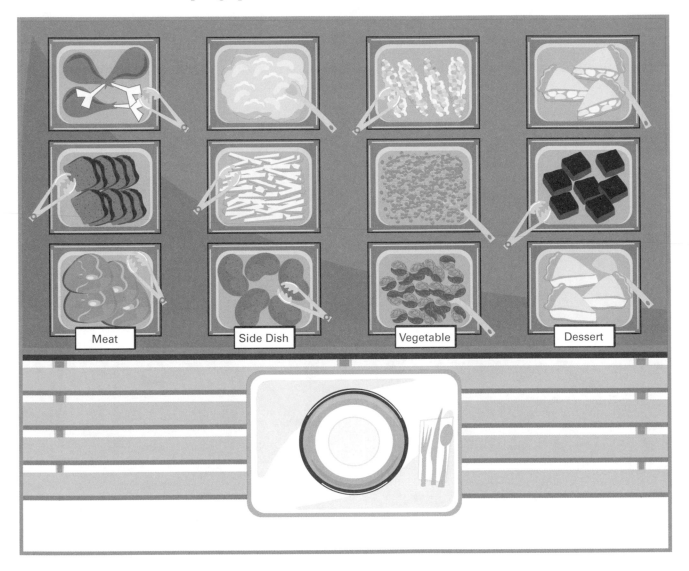

Meat   Side Dish   Vegetable   Dessert

Each time you go to the buffet, your plate should have a choice of one meat, one side dish, one vegetable, and one dessert. How many times can you visit the buffet and get a different plate of food?

_____ times

Bus Ride

READ the clues, and CIRCLE the answer.

The Gallagher sisters always sit together.
Andrew sits next to Alyssa and behind Bill.
Stella likes to sit in back.
Bill always takes the window seat next to Nolan.
Kayley sits in front of Becky.
Dan sits in the aisle seat next to Ella.

Where is Dan in this picture?

In the Neighborhood

WRITE the name of each family on the correct mailbox.

The Green family chose their house for its color.

The Park family is always complaining about the noise coming from the Taguchi house next door.

The Simpsons live across the street from the Green family.

The Taguchis don't like looking out their front window at the Links' lawn flamingoes.

The Meyers live between the Links and the Simpsons.

Colorful Campground

Each tent is a different color. READ the clues, and COLOR each tent red, blue, yellow, green, orange, or purple.

The blue tent is west of the road.

The orange tent is below the lake.

The purple tent is north of the green tent.

The tent farthest south is not orange or purple.

The tent closest to the lake is green.

The red tent has a view of the entire campground.

19 Distant Places

DRAW lines between the four pairs of towns that have a 20-mile stretch of road between them.

HINT: Use the map key to help you.

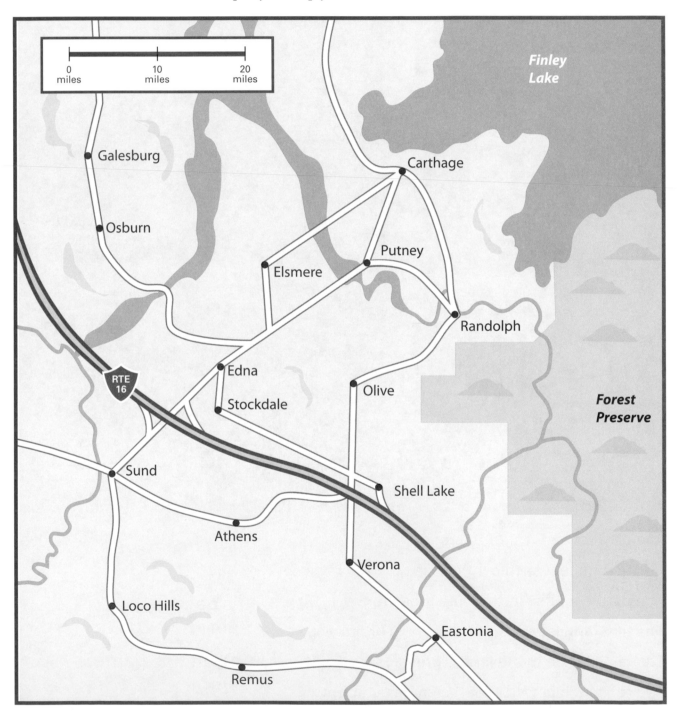

Flip a Coin

Probability is used to describe the chance of something happening. It can be represented by a number from 0 to 1.

Example: The probability that you will grow to be 30 feet tall is 0.

The probability that the sun will rise tomorrow morning is 1.

The probability of getting heads on a coin flip is $\frac{1}{2}$.

To see how probability works, try playing this game. FLIP a coin three times, and WRITE whether you flip heads or tails. SCORE 20 points for turns where you flip either three heads or three tails. SCORE 8 points for turns where you flip heads, heads, tails or tails, tails, heads. SCORE 5 points for any other coin combination. REPEAT this three more times. Then ANSWER the questions.

1	2	3	Score

1	2	3	Score

1	2	3	Score

1	2	3	Score

Total Score: _____

1. What is the chance of scoring 80 points in this game?
   impossible unlikely   likely   certain

2. What is the chance of scoring 15 points in this game?
   impossible unlikely   likely   certain

3. What is the chance of scoring at least 20 points in this game?
   impossible unlikely   likely   certain

21

Holding Hands

In one day, how many times do the hour and minute hands cross each other on a clock? WRITE the answer.

HINT: After 12:00, the first time that the clock hands cross each other is around 1:06. Think about what times the clock hands cross, and draw them on the clock to help you count. Try using a watch if you get stuck.

_____ times

Pocket Change

DRAW three straight lines to create six different money sets of equal value.

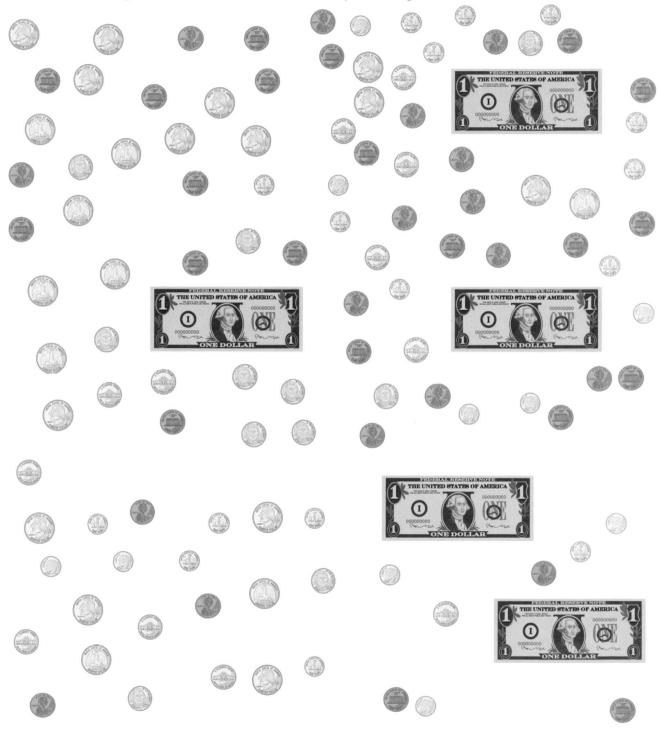

What's in My Hand?

READ the clues, and WRITE how many of each coin and bill are hidden in the hand.

I'm holding six paper bills and nine coins.

The money in my hand totals $48.89.

My coins total less than one dollar.

I don't have any 10-dollar bills.

What's in my hand?

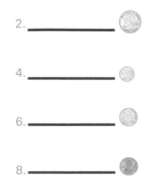

1. _____

2. _____

3. _____

4. _____

5. _____

6. _____

7. _____

8. _____

Section 3:
Vacation Challenge
Games & Activities

Contents

Tips for Summer Reading Success

- **Read often and everywhere.** Read in bed. Read on the couch. Read in the car, on the grass, and at the beach. Read in the bathtub! Sometimes the more unusual the place, the more fun kids will have reading.

- **Let your children see you reading.** Set a good example by the modeling the behavior you want to see. Have lots of books, magazines, and newspapers around the house, and set aside time where the whole family turns off the TV, puts down their phones, and picks up a book!

- **Be a word detective.** Point out the relationship between words and talk about how certain words have similar meanings or similar spellings.

- **Be regular library patron.** Heading to the library on a regular basis is a great way for kids to see that reading is a part of life, and not just a "school" activity. Let your child pick out books she is interested in, or ask the librarian for recommendations on what's popular with kids in her age group.

- **Make sure your child is reading a "just right" book.** If a book is too hard or too easy, then your child won't gain the fluency, comprehension, and confidence needed to make significant progress.

- **Listen and play off of your child's reading interests.** At this age, your child may already have established likes and dislikes in their reading material. Seek out books with a connection to those he already likes, such as further titles in a series or other books by the same author. You can also extend your child's genre "range" this way—for instance, if he enjoyed a novel about riding, you could look for a nonfiction book about horses!

- **Discuss books, both during and after you read.** Talk with your child about traits of story characters, problems and solutions, the lessons in texts, and important ideas or concepts featured in the books you've just read. These discussions are some of the best ways to help your child absorb and engage with literature!

Reading Extension Activities

Embark on an awesome adventure this summer with these creative activities. Each one helps foster critical thinking and reading comprehension skills.

Movie Advertising Mogul.

Bring a book to the big screen by designing a series of movie posters for it! Think about movie posters you've seen in real life—they focus on different parts of the story and the characters in order to appeal to different people. Design a poster for each of the four story elements: plot, setting, character, and theme.

Billboard Brainstorm.

Create a billboard to represent a book you've read and loved! Include the title and the author, then use your creativity to design a billboard that would make other people want to read that book. For instance, you could draw one or more of the characters or the setting; brainstorm and write words that describe the book; make a fun map of the story; or draw a symbol that represents the book's theme. What kind of images and information would make you want to pick up this book?

Summer Scrapbook.

Throughout your entire summer break, collect souvenirs of your family's summer activities, such as postcards of places you visited, ticket stubs for movies or shows you saw, and photographs of friends and family you visited. Get a big notebook and tape or glue in all of your souvenirs, then write captions that describe each image or event.

What's the News?

Pick a book you enjoyed reading and write a newscast all about it, starring YOU as the host of the evening news! Try to include at least three or four news segments. For instance, you could write:

- "headline" news (based on the story's problem and solution)

- an interview or profile (related to the characters or parts in the story)

- the weather (pertaining to the setting)

- a commercial or ad that would relate to the book!

When you're done writing, ask one of your parents to record you "broadcasting" the news.

Vigorous Vocabulary Words

Try using these challenging words in conversation with your child. Hearing new words in context is a great way to learn new words and remember what they mean. You can also treat these as sight words, and select a few words at a time from the list below to practice each day.

accomplish	critical	evidence	observe	result
adaptation	decrease	example	obvious	scarce
approached	defend	except	organized	select
argued	demonstrate	exclaimed	passage	separate
automatically	describe	experiment	persuade	simplify
avoid	detail	flexible	predict	summarize
border	develop	fortunate	prediction	support
calculate	difference	frequent	prefer	surround
cause	disappointed	furious	previous	temporary
circular	distribute	increasing	purpose	threatens
compare	effective	infer	rarely	tradition
concluding	eliminate	inform	reason	typical
confirm	entirety	insert	recognize	usually
contrast	essential	maximum	recommend	yield
convince	estimate	minimum	represent	zone

Try this activity to make practicing vocabulary fun!

Conversation Competition.
Pick a set of 10 vocabulary words from the list above. Then, challenge your child to talk with you for three minutes on a topic of her choice. The challenge is for her to correctly use as many of the 10 vocabulary words as possible during the three minutes! If she uses all 10, she becomes the Conversation Champ!

Summer Reading Mystery Picture

Can you complete the mystery picture before the summer ends? Each time you read a book, determine the genre it belongs to and color in one of the puzzle pieces that corresponds to the genre's number. (TIP: Some books belong to more than one genre!)

1. Fantasy
2. Realistic Fiction
3. Mystery
4. Science Fiction
5. Historical Fiction
6. Reference
7. Biography
8. Poetry
9. Fairy Tale
10. Folklore

Tips for Summer Math Success

- **Practice math with your child every day!** Like playing a sport or an instrument, you need to practice math often in order to improve. Catch a few minutes whenever you can during the day to do math. Whether at home, at the store, or in the car, opportunities for math are all around us.

- **Give your child a story problem to solve.** Have your child explain how to solve the problem. Add a fun twist by using names of movie stars, famous athletes, or musicians to pique her interest.

- **Cook with your child.** Let your child choose a recipe and help you shop for the ingredients. Then, he can take the lead when it comes to reading the directions, counting, measuring, and setting the timer.

- **Set up a summer store.** Buy a handful of small items or gather treasures that were already in the house (such as pencils, gum, Post-it Notes, stickers, and small candies). Give each item a price tag and have your child come to the store every few days to "buy" an item using coins and bills (or play money).

- **Playing games counts!** Games are often naturally filled with math. Capitalize on the math skills that are offered in board games and use those times of play to develop skills and extend your child's thinking. For example, Yahtzee works with basic addition and Battleship utilizes coordinate graphs. Puzzles encourage spatial awareness, and most card games build on concepts like greatest/least, addition/subtraction, or multiplication.

"Magic" Math

It's not magic—it's just math! These magnificent tricks work every time. See for yourself, then impress your friends with your mastery of mathematical "magic."

The Palindrome Trick.

A palindrome is a number that reads the same forward and backward, such as "2992." Follow the steps below to learn the trick to finding palindromes!

1. Write a three-digit number.

2. Reverse the digits (write it backwards), and add both numbers together.

3. Continue this process until you get a palindrome.

The Reappearing Number Trick.

Ask a friend to choose any four digits and follow these directions. The same number will appear every time.

1. Choose four different digits from 0–9.

2. Arrange the digits to make the largest possible number. Arrange the digits again to make the smallest possible number. Subtract the smaller number from the larger number.

3. Arrange the individual digits in the resulting answer to make the largest and smallest possible numbers. Subtract the numbers as before.

4. Continue the process in the same manner. Eventually you will arrive at the number 6174. No matter what four digits you choose, the number 6174 will always appear!

Marvelous Math Activities

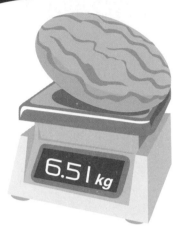

Estimate the Weight.

For this activity, find a selection of common fruits and vegetables. Ask your child to line them up in the order she thinks will be the lightest to heaviest. Then weigh each one to determine if her predictions were correct, and rearrange them if not! You can cut open each fruit or veggie to prompt a discussion about how density affects weight—and, of course, enjoy a healthy snack together when you're done.

Catalog Calculations.

Using a store catalog or ad section featuring kids' clothing, tell your child he's in charge of shopping for his own school clothes this year—but that he has to stay within budget! Give him a dollar amount that represents his budget, and challenge him to select a wardrobe form the catalog, while getting as close as he can to, but not exceeding, the budget. Every cent counts! As a challenge, you can set additional parameters, such as those below:

- Include specific numbers of items (such as 2 pairs of pants, 5 shirts, and 1 jacket)

- Include multiples of the same item in different colors

- If he has a 20% discount coupon, how much money will he save? How many more items can he add to his order with that saved money?

Sports Statistics.

Crumple a piece of scrap paper or newspaper up to make a "basketball," and set a trash bin five or ten feet away. Taking turns, you and your child should try to shoot the basketball into the bin 10 times each, recording your success or failure each time. Once you're done, ask your child to figure out the ratios of success and failure for each of you. Then help your child convert each ratio into its decimal form.

Decimal Card Decks.

Create a place value mat on a piece of paper for each person playing (2 to 5 players), with 5 columns and a decimal after the third column (for the hundreds, tens, ones, tenths, and hundredths places). Remove the tens, Jokers, and face cards from a card deck, then ask your child to shuffle the deck and deal 5 cards to each player. When you say "Go!", each player arranges their cards to create the largest number possible, then records that number on their place value mat. Whoever has the largest number gets a point—and after five rounds, whoever has the most points wins!

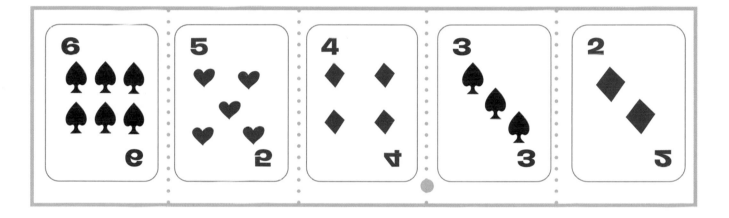

Edible Engineering.

All you need are pretzel sticks and marshmallows for some delicious engineering practice! Using the marshmallows as corner pieces, build three-dimensional shapes with the pretzel sticks. Your child can start with cubes and pyramids, then build more advanced structures such as a house with one or more floors. Assuming each pretzel stick equals 1 unit, ask your child to calculate the area and perimeter of each of the faces of one of their 3-D structures.

Independent Activities!

These independent activities can be completed by rising fifth graders with minimal parental involvement!

Mock Interview. Write the names of famous people from history on slips of paper and put them in a basket. Choose one at a time and challenge yourself to come up with questions that you would ask that person if you were doing a newspaper interview with him or her. Make sure you know why that person is considered famous, and do some research if needed. Here are some ideas: Amelia Earhart, Betsy Ross, Paul Revere, Benjamin Franklin, Martin Luther King, Jr., Susan B. Anthony, and John F. Kennedy.

What Am I? This is a geography activity that you can play anytime, even on the go. Ask a parent or guardian to prepare a list of "places in the world" and challenge yourself to identify whether each one would be categorized as a city, state, country or continent. Here is a list to get you started: Chicago, Arizona, Paris, Africa, Moscow, Australia, Detroit, Spain, Idaho, Asia, Vermont, Toronto, Argentina, Egypt, and Tokyo. (It can be useful to have a globe or map handy!)

"All About Me" Tee

Decorate the T-shirt below to reflect YOU—your passions and your interests! Have fun planning what to write and draw in each section. Here are some ideas for the sections (you can use as many or few as you want): self-portrait, family members and their names, favorite subject in school, best friend(s), favorite food, favorite song, favorite movie, favorite sport and/or sports team, favorite color, favorite animal, words to describe you, favorite book.

If you feel extra inspired, you can use fabric markers and an old white T-shirt to create your design in real life!

Beach Bums

This game is endlessly adaptable. Mark a set of index cards with skills you'd like your child to practice or try some of the suggestions below! Then PICK a skill card set (or SHUFFLE the cards together) to practice. READ the rules. PLAY the game!

- Determine place value to the millions

- Describe the characteristics of different book genres

- Round numbers to the nearest thousand, ten thousand, hundred thousand, and million

- Add and subtract fractions with common denominators

- Correctly identify the parts of a book

- Convert basic fractions to decimals and vice versa

- Read, write, and spell vocabulary words

- Determine if an angle is right, acute, or obtuse

- Identify 3D shapes and name the number of faces, edges, and vertices

Rules: Two players

1. Place your skill cards in a face-down stack. Place the playing pieces on the Start space.

2. Take turns rolling a number cube and picking a skill card.

3. If you correctly complete the task on the skill card, you can move forward the number of spaces on the number cube.

4. If you land on a space with a number, move the number of spaces in the direction the arrow indicates. If you land on a space with a starfish, take another turn!

The first player to the beach towel wins!

Shape Scavenging

Use these scorecards, and go on a shape scavenger hunt. READ the rules. PLAY the game!

Rules: Two players or teams

1. Pick a location and a time limit for your scavenger hunt. For example, your scavenger hunt can be inside the house for 20 minutes, or each player can pick a different room.
2. When you find something that has the same shape as the shapes on the scorecards, write its name. Shapes that are harder to find earn more points.
3. At the end of the scavenger hunt, add up your points.

The player or team with the most points wins!

| Rectangular prism: 5 points | Cylinder: 8 points | Sphere: 10 points |
| Cube: 12 points | Cone: 15 points | Square pyramid: 20 points |

PLAYER 1

	Items Found	Points
	Total Points	

PLAYER 2

	Items Found	Points
	Total Points	

Questions and discussion are a pivotal part of reading. Take time to pose questions and engage in book discussions with your child to help build valuable reading comprehension skills. The prompts below are good ways to get the conversation started!

Before Reading:

• Based on the cover and title, what do you think this book will be about?

• What makes you think that?

• What characters do you think might be in our story?

• Do you think there will be a problem in this story? Why or why not?

• Does the topic/story relate to you or your family? How?

During Reading:

• What do you think will happen next? Why?

• What emotions is the character feeling? How do you know?

• Has anything like this ever happened to you? Does it remind you of something?

• Do you know someone like this character?

• Can you put what you've just read into your own words?

After Reading:

- In your opinion, were the title and cover good matches for this book?

- Were your predictions about the story correct?

- Retell the most important events in the story from beginning, middle, and end.

- What is the main message of this book? What does the author want you to know?

- If this story had a sequel, what do you think it would be about?

- If you could change one thing in the story, what would it be?

- Why do you think the author wanted to write this book?

Use the P.I.C.K. acronym to help select a "just right" book.

P	Purpose	Why do I want to read this book? Am I reading for fun, to learn, or another reason?
I	Interest	Am I interested in the subject of this book? If not, does it have connections to things I am interested in?
C	Comprehend	Do I understand the words? Is the subject something I "get"?
K	Know the Words	Do I know how to read most of the words? If there are more than 4 unknown words on a page, this book might be too difficult right now.

Recommended Reading List

These books are full of interesting plotlines, relatable characters, and "just right" stories for young bookworms reading on their own. Asterisks indicate the start of a recommended series.

Home of the Brave by Katherine Applegate

Poppy* by Avi

Tuck Everlasting by Natalie Babbitt

A Bear Named Trouble by Marion Dane Bauer

Bud, Not Buddy by Christopher Paul Curtis

The Tale of Despereaux by Kate DiCamillo

How to Train Your Dragon* by Cressida Cowell

Ginger Pye by Eleanor Estes

Harriet the Spy* by Louise Fitzhugh

Fig Pudding by Ralph Fletcher

My Side of the Mountain by Jean Craighead George

The Talent Show by Dan Gutman

Inside Out and Back Again by Thanhha Lai

A Dog's Life by Ann M. Martin

Shadow by Michael Morpurgo

Big Nate* by Lincoln Pierce

Scary Tales* by James Preller

The Lightning Thief* by Rick Riordan

Harry Potter and the Sorcerer's Stone* by J.K. Rowling

The Van Gogh Cafe by Cynthia Rylant

The Cricket in Times Square* by George Selden

My Life as a Book* by Janet Tashjian

You're the Critic

Pick some of your favorite (or least favorite) books and write a review for each. Color in the number of stars you'd give each book!

Book 1 Title: _____

Book 1 Author: _____

My Review: ☆☆☆☆☆ _____

_____

_____

Book 2 Title: _____

Book 2 Author: _____

My Review: ☆☆☆☆☆ _____

_____

_____

Book 3 Title: _____

Book 3 Author: _____

My Review: ☆☆☆☆☆ _____

_____

_____

Recommended Math Reading List

Books provide many fantastic opportunities to reinforce math concepts, whether through narrative text or illustrations. Here are some great reads that help develop math skills.

Math Chapter Books

Chasing Vermeer by Blue Balliett

Lunch Money by Andrew Clements

The Lemonade War by Jacqueline Davies

The Number Devil by Hans Magnus Enzensberger

The Candy Corn Contest by Patricia Reilly Giff

The Phantom Tollbooth by Norton Juster

The Toothpaste Millionaire by Jean Merrill

The Adventures of Penrose the Mathematical Cat by Theoni Pappas

A Grain of Rice by Helena Clare Pittman

Sideways Arithmetic from Wayside School by Louis Sachar

Math Picture Books

Multiplying Menace by Pam Calvert

Sir Cumference and the Roundabout Battle by Cindy Neuschwander

G is for Googol by David M. Schwartz

Math Curse by Jon Scieszka

The Grapes of Math by Greg Tang

Math-terpieces by Greg Tang

You're the Critic

Pick some of your favorite (or least favorite) math books and write a review for each. Color in the number of stars you'd give each book!

Book 1 Title:

Book 1 Author:

My Review: ☆☆☆☆☆

Book 2 Title:

Book 2 Author:

My Review: ☆☆☆☆☆

Book 3 Title:

Book 3 Author:

My Review: ☆☆☆☆☆

Page 58

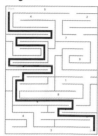

7,138,605

Page 59

1. 84,165	2. 4,672,244
3. 961,723	4. 29,811
5. 115,736	6. 2,082,641
7. 505,692	8. 3,937,260

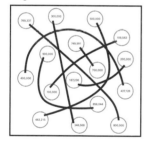

Page 60

1. 228,864	2. 341,156
3. 275,319	4. 384,620
5. 382,495	6. 392,382
7. 232,981	8. 337,236
9. 246,518	

Page 61

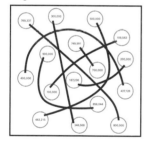

Page 62

1. 5,237,564	2. 5,418,163
3. 5,908,752	4. 6,692,556
5. 6,694,204	6. 6,563,827
7. 5,879,215	8. 5,418,921
9. 5,826,138	

Page 63

1. 4, 5   2. 2, 7   3. 5, 3

Page 64

1,839,617

Page 65

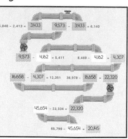

Page 66

1. 76,977	2. 85,543
3. 51,349	4. 59,868
5. 99,758	6. 62,372
7. 40,703	8. 71,230

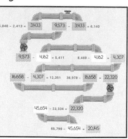

Page 67

Page 68

1. 22,311	2. 76,213
3. 55,224	4. 71,018
5. 49,876	6. 18,236
7. 61,086	8. 34,972

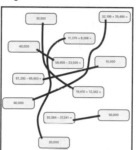

Page 69

Page 70

Page 71

1. 30	2. 16	3. 36
4. 25	5. 21	6. 60
7. 7	8. 72	9. 48
10. 18	11. 45	12. 40

WHEREVER YOU PUT HIM.

Page 72

	4	7
1	4	7
2	8	14

	5	6
1	5	6
3	15	18

	2	7
9	18	63
10	20	70

	5	8
2	10	16
6	30	48

	3	8
7	21	56
9	27	72

	5	6
7	35	42
9	45	54

Page 73

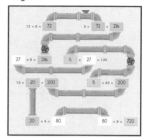

Page 74

13	×	11	=	143
×		×		×
6	×	14	=	84
=		=		=
78	×	154	=	12,012

Page 75

1. 7	2. 8	3. 10
4. 1	5. 4	6. 2
7. 5	8. 1	9. 3
10. 12	11. 6	12. 9

HE CAUGHT A LOT OF FLIES.

Page 76

1. 9, 2, 6, 8
2. 8, 3, 1, 7
3. 16, 4, 8, 10

Page 77

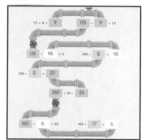

Page 78

972	÷	36	=	27
÷		÷		÷
54	÷	6	=	9
=		=		=
18	÷	6	=	3

Answers

Page 79
1. SU   2. M   3. ME
4. R   5. VAC   6. A
7. TI   8. ON
SUMMER VACATION

Page 80
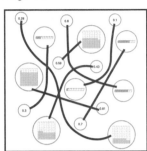

Page 81
1. $\frac{3}{4}$ 2. $\frac{5}{6}$ 3. $\frac{3}{3}$

4. $\frac{5}{9}$ 5. $\frac{7}{8}$ 6. $\frac{2}{5}$

7. $\frac{2}{3}$ 8. $\frac{5}{8}$ 9. $\frac{5}{7}$

THE LIBRARY.

Page 82
1. $\frac{1}{6}$, $\frac{2}{6}$, $\frac{3}{6}$, $\frac{4}{6}$

2. $\frac{1}{8}$, $\frac{3}{8}$, $\frac{5}{8}$, $\frac{6}{8}$

3. $\frac{1}{12}$, $\frac{4}{12}$, $\frac{6}{12}$, $\frac{8}{12}$,

Page 83
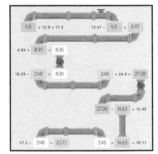

Page 84
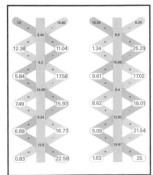

Page 85
A FENCE.

Page 86
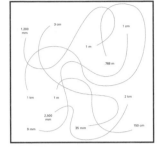

Page 87
A JUNKYARD.

Page 88
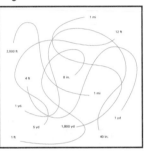

Page 89
Have someone check your answers.

Page 90
Have someone check your answers.

Page 91
1. 5,000   2. 2.3   3. 6,000
4. 0.6   5. 3   6. 6,500
7. 1,500   8. 10.4   9. 200
10. 1
YOU CAN ADD A HOLE.

Page 92
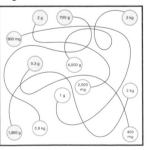

Page 93
1. 2   2. $1\frac{1}{2}$ 3. 32

4. 500   5. 6,000   6. $2\frac{1}{2}$

7. 1   8. 12   9. 8

10. 5,500

THEY BOTH WEIGH ONE TON.

Page 94
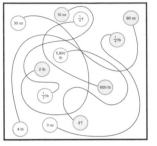

Page 95

Page 96

Page 97
144

Page 98
81

Page 99

Page 100
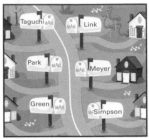

Page 101

Page 102

Page 103
1. unlikely
2. impossible
3. certain

Page 104
22 (Clock hands pass each other around the times 1:06, 2:11, 3:17, 4:22, 5:27, 6:33, 7:38, 8:43, 9:49, 10:55, and 12:00 twice per day.)

Page 105
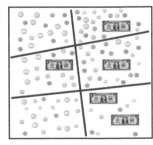

Page 106
1. 2   2. 3
3. 0   4. 0
5. 1   6. 2
7. 3   8. 4

I'M SUMMER SMART!

This award is presented to

on

for a great job finishing the
**Sylvan Summer Smart:
Between Grades
4 & 5 Workbook!**

Sylvan
Learning℠

adequate

Make sure to leave *adequate* room for dessert.

amuse

Though the first act of the play might bore you, the second one will definitely *amuse* you

artificial

The *artificial* tree looked so good, I had to touch it to know for sure it wasn't real.

attract

Jen thought her perfume would *attract* boys, but it really smelled like dirty socks!

binoculars

Our seats were a long way from the racetrack, but I used my *binoculars* to pick out my favorite car.

capable

After training for several months, Sasha felt *capable* of running the marathon.

charity

Jesse is raising money for a *charity* that finds homes for stray pets.

clutch

During the scary movie, my little sister had to *clutch* my hand because she was scared.

conduct

Before the kids toured the art museum, they were instructed on the rules and proper *conduct* while inside.

ad·e·quate

AD-ih-kwiht

adjective
enough to satisfy

a·muse

uh-MYOOZ

verb
1. to charm or entertain
2. to make smile or laugh

ar·ti·fi·cial

ahr-tuh-FIHSH-uhl

adjective
unnatural; man-made

at·tract

uh-TRAKT

verb
to pull something toward something else

bin·oc·u·lars

buh-NAHK-yuh-lerz

noun
a magnifying device with two lenses
for seeing faraway objects

ca·pa·ble

KAY-puh-buhl

adjective
having the ability to accomplish a specific task

char·i·ty

CHAR-ih-tee

noun
1. an organization or institution created to
help the needy or promote a cause
2. something given to help a person in need

clutch

kluhch

verb
to hold tightly; snatch

con·duct

KAHN-duhkt

noun
the way a person acts

convertible

Sasha's toy was a *convertible* bulldozer that could turn into an action hero.

decisive

When it was time to choose between chocolate cake and apple pie, Lila was *decisive*.

device

A hearing aid is a *device* that some people wear in their ears to help them hear sounds more clearly.

enable

The money Mom included with her letter will *enable* me to buy some snacks at the camp trading post.

equator

The Earth is hottest near the *equator*.

expedition

To cool off in the heat of the summer, Jonas imagines himself on an arctic *expedition*.

frequent

I made *frequent* trips to the mailbox when I was waiting for my package to arrive.

garment

As the queen moved, her *garment* flowed behind her like a sparkling river.

gravity

Astronauts can float around because *gravity* has less of an effect in outer space than it does on Earth.

con•vert•i•ble

kuhn-VER-tuh-buhl

adjective
able to change in form

de•ci•sive

dih-SI-sihv

adjective
having the power to make firm decisions

de•vice

dih-VIS

noun
an instrument that serves a specific purpose

en•a•ble

ehn-AY-buhl

verb
to make possible

e•qua•tor

ih-KWAY-ter

noun
an imaginary line drawn around the middle of the Earth

ex•pe•di•tion

ehk-spih-DIHSH-uhn

noun
1. a journey or trip taken for a specific purpose
2. an organized group undertaking such a journey

fre•quent

FREE-kwuhnt

adjective
occurring often or regularly

gar•ment

GAHR-muhnt

noun
a piece of clothing

grav•i•ty

GRAV-ih-tee

noun
1. the force that pulls things toward the center of the Earth
2. seriousness

harmony

Everyone got along, and there was *harmony* at the sleepover.

hydrant

Toby's dog always makes a beeline for that fire *hydrant*.

immortal

Fairy tales are *immortal* stories that will be told as long as there are children to hear them.

inspire

I hope my new cookie recipe will *inspire* a lot of customers to buy them at the fair.

interstate

To get from Pennsylvania to Ohio, we took an *interstate* highway.

keen

Lydia has a *keen* interest in horses.

linger

Carla likes to *linger* at the end of a movie to see the final credits.

marvel

My cousin thinks everything his new puppy does is a *marvel*.

mischief

Sometimes when the dogs are alone, they shred the newspaper and get into other *mischief*.

har·mo·ny
HAHR-muh-nee
noun
1. agreement, peace, and unity
2. in music, a combination of tones

hy·drant
HI-druhnt
noun
a pipe for drawing water from a main pipe

im·mor·tal
ih-MOR-tuhl
adjective
1. remembered forever
2. living forever

in·spire
ihn-SPIR
verb
to cause an uplifting feeling or thought

in·ter·state
IHN-ter-stayt
adjective
between two or more states

keen
keen
adjective
1. intense or strongly felt
2. very sharp, as a knife

lin·ger
LIHNG-ger
verb
to remain or stay on in a place longer than is needed

mar·vel
MAHR-vuhl
noun
something that causes awe or wonder
verb
to be filled with awe or wonder

mis·chief
MIHS-chihf
noun
teasing or playful behavior that causes annoyance

musical

I can't carry a tune, but my brother is very *musical*.

noticeable

Abby hoped the stain on her skirt wasn't too *noticeable*.

organize

Pete liked to *organize* all his video games so he'd know if his brother took one.

paradise

The theme park we're going to is advertised as a "kid's *paradise*."

plunge

It was so hot outside, Owen couldn't wait to *plunge* into the cool lake.

portion

Eliza only watched a *portion* of the TV show because it was time for bed.

protection

Shawn put his cell phone in a sturdy case for extra *protection* in case he dropped it.

quiver

Our little dog will *quiver* and hide under the bed whenever she hears thunder.

report

I brought my umbrella because the weather *report* said that it would rain.

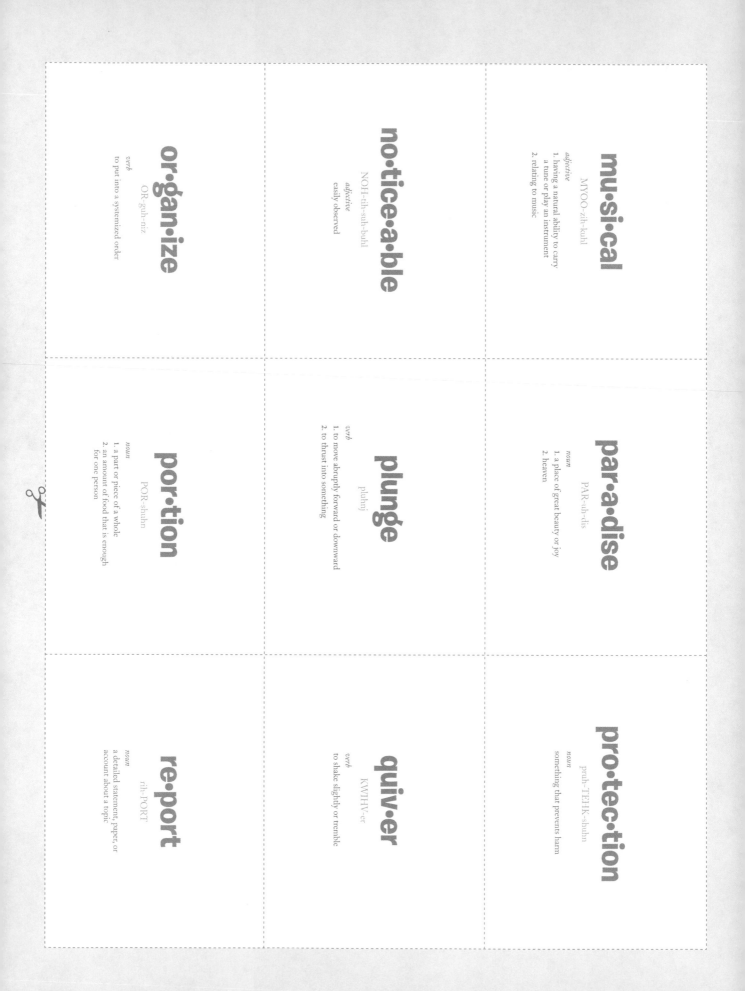

mu·si·cal
MYOO-zih-kuhl

adjective
1. having a natural ability to carry a tune or play an instrument
2. relating to music

par·a·dise
PAR-uh-dis

noun
1. a place of great beauty or joy
2. heaven

pro·tec·tion
pruh-TEHK-shuhn

noun
something that prevents harm

no·tice·a·ble
NOH-tih-suh-buhl

adjective
easily observed

plunge
pluhnj

verb
1. to move abruptly forward or downward
2. to thrust into something

quiv·er
KWIHV-er

verb
to shake slightly or tremble

or·gan·ize
OR-guh-niz

verb
to put into a systemized order

por·tion
POR-shuhn

noun
1. a part or piece of a whole
2. an amount of food that is enough for one person

re·port
rih-PORT

noun
a detailed statement, paper, or account about a topic

scamper

Sometimes at night, I can hear an animal *scamper* across the attic floor.

shallow

Vera learned to swim in the *shallow* end of the pool.

stagger

When I get off the tire swing, I always *stagger* for a few minutes until I regain my balance.

thermometer

The *thermometer* showed the temperature to be hotter than normal.

tremendous

A *tremendous* crack of thunder woke me up in the middle of the night.

urge

I *urge* you to try playing lacrosse if you ever get the chance.

vertical

When I startled my cat, she did a crazy *vertical* leap.

vow

Paula made a *vow* to her dad that she would always ask before using his tools.

report

I brought my umbrella because the weather *report* said that it would rain.

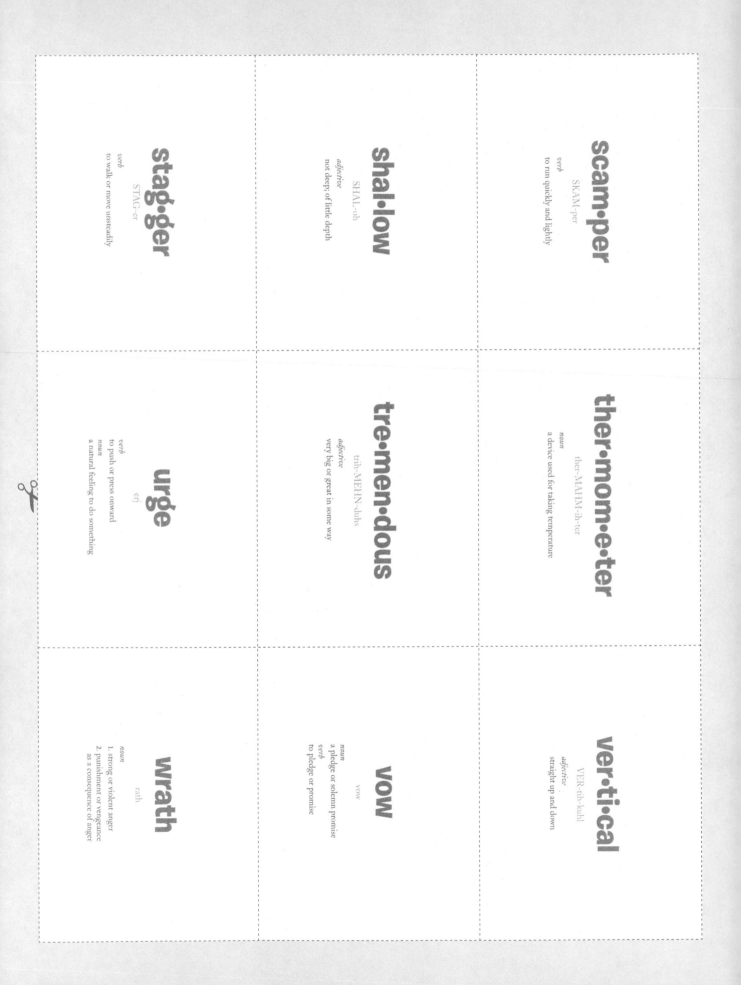

scam·per

SKAM-per

verb
to run quickly and lightly

shal·low

SHAL-oh

adjective
not deep; of little depth

stag·ger

STAG-er

verb
to walk or move unsteadily

ther·mom·e·ter

ther-MAHM-ih-ter

noun
a device used for taking temperature

tre·men·dous

trih-MEHN-duhs

adjective
very big or great in some way

urge

erj

verb
to push or press onward
noun
a natural feeling to do something

ver·ti·cal

VER-tih-kuhl

adjective
straight up and down

vow

vow

noun
a pledge or solemn promise
verb
to pledge or promise

wrath

rath

noun
1. strong or violent anger
2. punishment or vengeance
   as a consequence of anger

Determine the place of each digit in the number.

8,523,762

Determine the place of each digit in the number.

1,994,857

Round the number to the nearest thousand.

4,603

Round the number to the nearest ten thousand.

83,723

Round the number to the nearest hundred thousand.

968,615

Round the number to the nearest million.

3,248,955

When fractions have the same denominator, add them by adding the numerators only. The denominator stays the same. Add the fractions and determine the sum.

$\frac{5}{9} + \frac{2}{9} =$

When fractions have the same denominator, add them by adding the numerators only. The denominator stays the same. Add the fractions and determine the sum.

$\frac{5}{8} + \frac{5}{8} =$

When fractions have the same denominator, add them by adding the numerators only. The denominator stays the same. Add the fractions and determine the sum.

$\frac{1}{7} + \frac{6}{7} =$

8 millions
5 hundred thousands
2 ten thousands
3 thousands
7 hundreds
6 tens
2 ones

1 millions
9 hundred thousands
9 ten thousands
4 thousands
8 hundreds
5 tens
7 ones

5,000

80,000

1,000,000

3,000,000

$$\frac{5}{9} + \frac{2}{9} = \frac{7}{9}$$

$$\frac{5}{8} + \frac{5}{8} = \frac{10}{8}$$

$$\frac{1}{7} + \frac{6}{7} = \frac{7}{7}$$

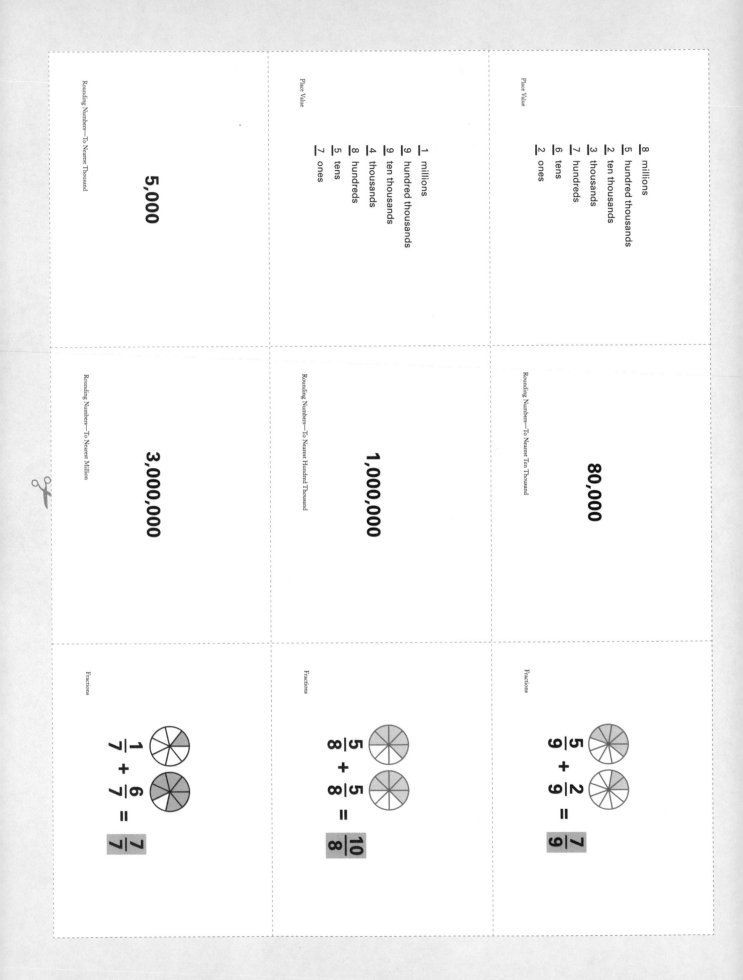

When fractions have the same denominator, subtract them by subtracting the numerators only. The denominator stays the same. Subtract the fractions and determine the difference.

$$\frac{3}{4} - \frac{1}{4} =$$

When fractions have the same denominator, subtract them by subtracting the numerators only. The denominator stays the same. Subtract the fractions and determine the difference.

$$\frac{7}{8} - \frac{2}{8} =$$

When fractions have the same denominator, subtract them by subtracting the numerators only. The denominator stays the same. Subtract the fractions and determine the difference.

$$\frac{6}{6} - \frac{5}{6} =$$

Determine the fraction and decimal for the picture.

Determine the fraction and decimal for the picture.

Determine the fraction and decimal for the picture.

Determine the fraction and decimal for the picture.

Decimals are used to represent dollars and cents. Determine the value of the money.

Decimals are used to represent dollars and cents. Determine the value of the money.

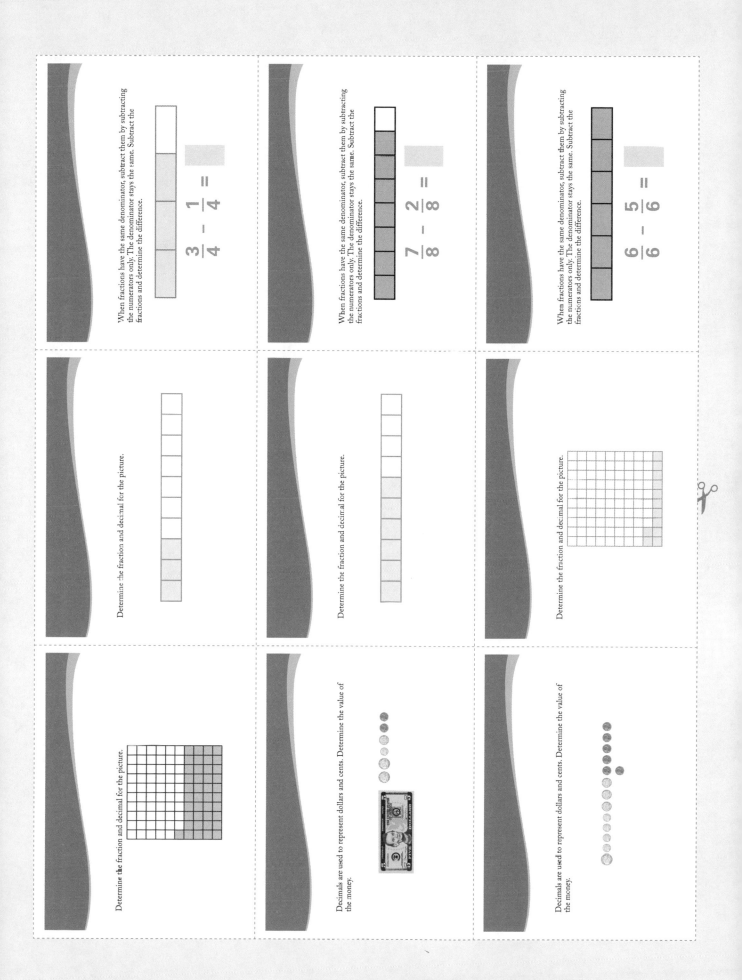

$$\frac{3}{4} - \frac{1}{4} = \frac{2}{4}$$

$$\frac{7}{8} - \frac{2}{8} = \frac{5}{8}$$

$$\frac{6}{6} - \frac{5}{6} = \frac{1}{6}$$

$$\frac{3}{10}, 0.3$$

$$\frac{6}{10}, 0.6$$

$$\frac{12}{100}, 0.12$$

$$\frac{41}{100}, 0.41$$

$5.67

$0.86

Decimals are used to represent dollars and cents. Determine the value of the money.

Determine if the decimal on the left is *greater than* (>), *less than* (<), or *equal to* (=) the decimal on the right.

0.4 ☐ 0.7

Determine if the decimal on the left is *greater than* (>), *less than* (<), or *equal to* (=) the decimal on the right.

1.4 ☐ 1.2

Determine if the decimal on the left is *greater than* (>), *less than* (<), or *equal to* (=) the decimal on the right.

1.3 ☐ 1.7

Determine the equivalent measurement.

6 m = ☐ cm

Determine the equivalent measurement.

12 cm = ☐ mm

Determine the equivalent measurement.

10 km = ☐ m

Determine the equivalent measurement.

2 ft = ☐ in.

Determine the equivalent measurement.

36 in. = ☐ ft

Decimals

Decimals

$7.09

Decimals

1.3 < 1.7

Measurement—Length

10 km = 10,000 m

Decimals

0.4 < 0.7

Measurement—Length

6 m = 600 cm

Measurement—Length

2 ft = 24 in.

Decimals

1.4 > 1.2

Measurement—Length

12 cm = 120 mm

Measurement—Length

36 in. = 3 ft

Determine the equivalent measurement.

1 yd = ☐ in.

Determine the name of the shape and the number of its sides and vertices.

Determine the name of the shape and the number of its sides and vertices.

Determine the name of the shape and the number of its sides and vertices.

Determine the number of right, acute, and obtuse angles in the shape.

Determine the number of right, acute, and obtuse angles in the shape.

Determine the number of right, acute, and obtuse angles in the shape.

Determine the name of the shape and the number of its vertices, edges, and faces.

Determine the name of the shape and the number of its vertices, edges, and faces.

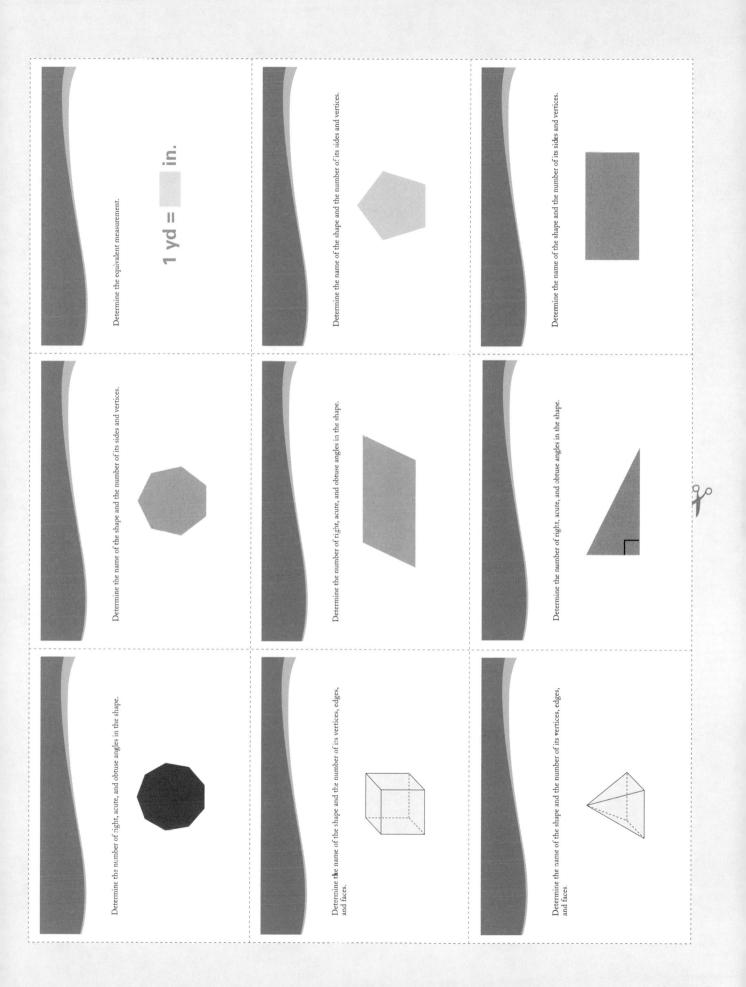

1 yd = 36 in.

Measurement—Length

heptagon
7 sides
7 vertices

Geometry—Plane Shapes

0 right angles
0 acute angles
9 obtuse angles

Geometry—Plane Shapes

pentagon
5 sides
5 vertices

Geometry—Plane Shapes

0 right angles
2 acute angles
2 obtuse angles

Geometry—Plane Shapes

cube

Vertices	Edges	Faces
8	12	6

Geometry—Solid Shapes

rectangle
4 sides
4 vertices

Geometry—Plane Shapes

1 right angle
2 acute angles
0 obtuse angles

Geometry—Plane Shapes

square pyramid

Vertices	Edges	Faces
5	8	5

Geometry—Solid Shapes

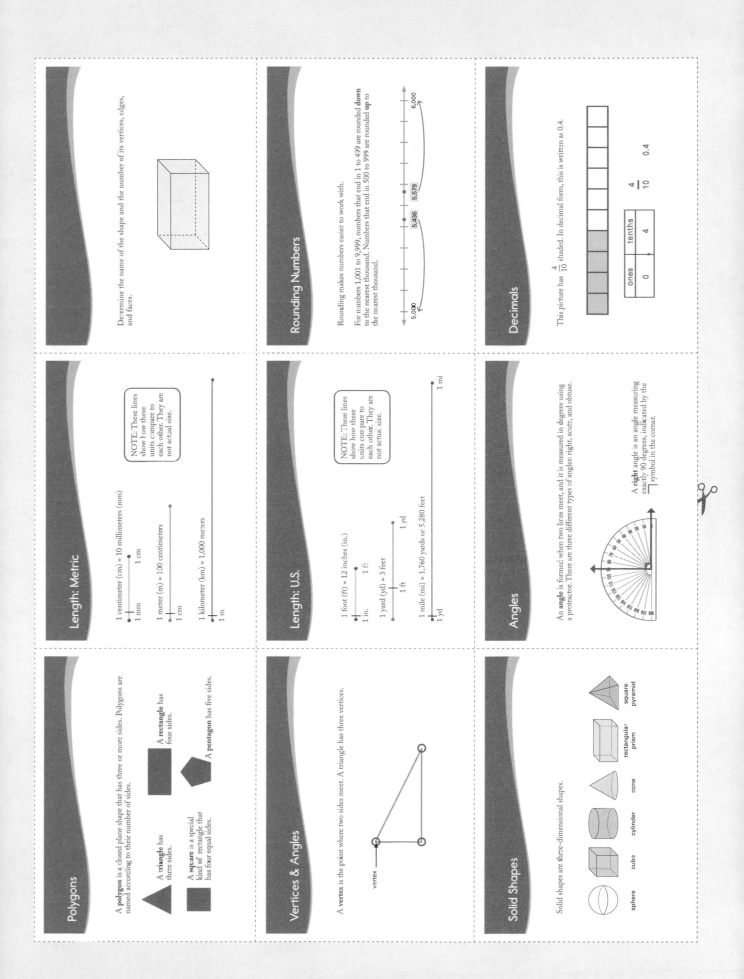

Determine the name of the shape and the number of its vertices, edges, and faces.

Rounding Numbers

Rounding makes numbers easier to work with.

For numbers 1,001 to 9,999, numbers that end in 1 to 499 are rounded **down** to the nearest thousand. Numbers that end in 500 to 999 are rounded **up** to the nearest thousand.

5,000   5,436   5,579   6,000

Decimals

This picture has $\frac{4}{10}$ shaded. In decimal form, this is written as 0.4.

ones		tenths
0	.	4

$\frac{4}{10}$

0.4

Length: Metric

1 centimeter (cm) = 10 millimeters (mm)
1 mm   1 cm

1 meter (m) = 100 centimeters
1 cm

1 kilometer (km) = 1,000 meters
1 m

NOTE: These lines show how these units compare to each other. They are not actual size.

Length: U.S.

1 foot (ft) = 12 inches (in.)
1 in.   1 ft.

1 yard (yd) = 3 feet
1 ft   1 yd

1 mile (mi) = 1,760 yards or 5,280 feet
1 yd   1 mi

NOTE: These lines show how these units compare to each other. They are not actual size.

Angles

An **angle** is formed when two lines meet, and it is measured in degrees using a protractor. There are three different types of angles: right, acute, and obtuse.

A **right** angle is an angle measuring exactly 90 degrees, indicated by the symbol in the corner.

Polygons

A **polygon** is a closed plane shape that has three or more sides. Polygons are named according to their number of sides.

A **triangle** has three sides.

A **rectangle** has four sides.

A **square** is a special kind of rectangle that has four equal sides.

A **pentagon** has five sides.

Vertices & Angles

A **vertex** is the point where two sides meet. A triangle has three vertices.

vertex

Solid Shapes

Solid shapes are three-dimensional shapes.

sphere   cube   cylinder   cone   rectangular prism   square pyramid

151

rectangular prism

Vertices	Edges	Faces
8	12	6

For numbers 10,001 to 99,999, numbers that end in 1 to 4,999 are rounded **down** to the nearest ten thousand. Numbers that end in 5,000 to 9,999 are rounded **up** to the nearest ten thousand.

For numbers 100,001 to 999,999, numbers that end in 1 to 49,999 are rounded **down** to the nearest hundred thousand. Numbers that end in 50,000 to 99,999 are rounded **up** to the nearest hundred thousand.

For numbers 1,000,001 to 9,999,999, numbers that end in 1 to 499,999 are rounded **down** to the nearest million. Numbers that end in 500,000 to 999,999 are rounded **up** to the nearest million.

This picture has $\frac{63}{100}$ shaded. In decimal form, this is written as 0.63.

ones	tenths	hundredths
0	6	3

$\frac{63}{100}$ 0.63

An **acute** angle is any angle measuring less than 90 degrees.

An **obtuse** angle is any angle measuring more than 90 degrees.

A **hexagon** has six sides.

An **octagon** has eight sides.

A **heptagon** has seven sides.

A **nonagon** has nine sides.

Two lines connected by a vertex form an angle. A square has four right angles.

In a three-dimensional shape, a **vertex** is where three or more edges meet. An **edge** is where two sides meet. A **face** is the shape formed by the edges.

Example:

vertices

face

edge

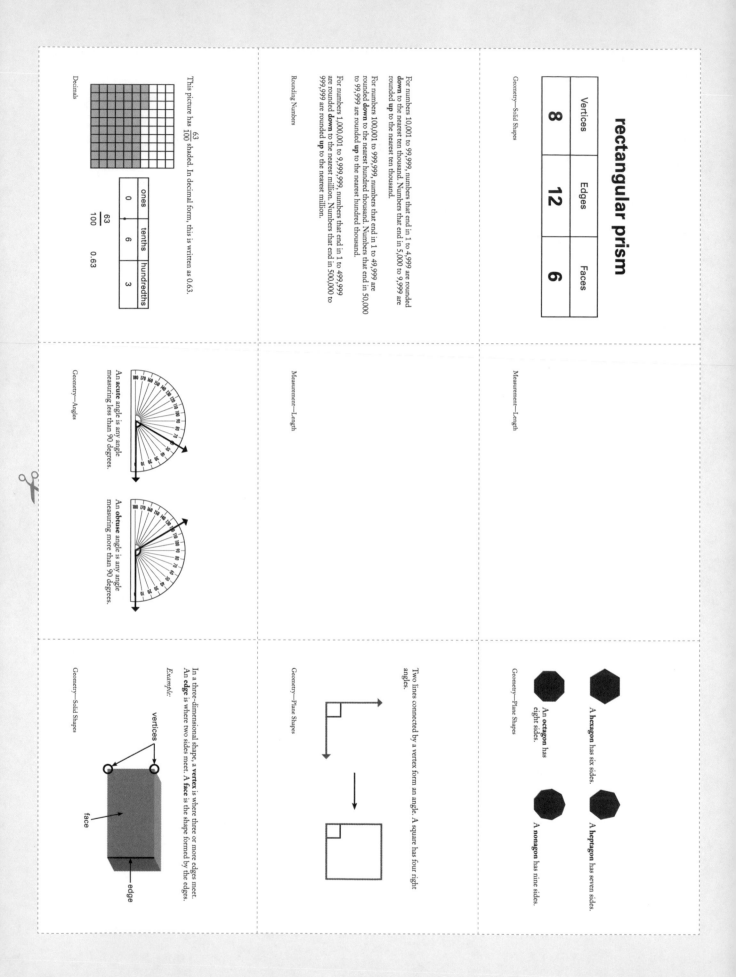

152